Majors and Minors for Graduates

Majors and Minors for Graduates

**Today's Choices
from the Prophets**

Brent D. Earles

BAKER BOOK HOUSE
Grand Rapids, Michigan 49516

For my friend and counselor,
Al Sarno,
who helped me see that God
still uses those who
"walk with a limp"

Contents

Prophecies of Catastrophe

(Jonah and Hosea)

Prophecies of Honor

(Amos and Micah)

Prophecies of Character

(Nahum, Zephaniah, and Habakkuk)

Prophecies of Perception

(Haggai and Zechariah)

Prophecies of Heart

(Malachi)

Introduction

I know some guys I want you to meet, but not just yet. Let's talk education first—probably the farthest thing from the mind of a graduate who wants to rest from the books for a while.

You're probably starting to think a little about life after high school. Some of you decided months ago what your major will be in college. Some of you decided to major in something besides college courses, and quite likely you're already busy with a full-time job. Good-bye books! And so-called higher education isn't for everyone, so that's okay.

Whatever group you fall into, your "majors and minors" in life are bound to change a few times over the next few years. I changed my college major three times before graduating with a Bachelor of Arts degree in Pastoral Counseling. Since then I've had three career changes. That's probably below average. So, if I were you, I wouldn't dig in my heels too deep. You might end up doing something you never dreamed of and love your career to pieces. Academic majors and minors have little to do with real education, anyway.

Boy, I bet the educators will love me for that one. Can't help it. The truth is, living has taught me more than any textbook ever did. I learned more about being a pastor in my first year of pastoring than I did in five years of intense study. I have a notion that's true of most professions—journalists, attorneys, doctors, and all the others. You know what they say, "Experience is the best teacher." Well, 'tis true.

Don't get me wrong. I'm all for formal majors and minors, B.A.'s, B.S.'s, A.A.'s, and all that degree talk. In fact, my preference is that every high school graduate invest at least one year in college, if at all possible. Attending college probably broadens one's understanding and perspective on life more than anything else a young adult can do. Nonetheless, you will grow more from living than from listening to lectures.

But life has lots of majors and minors that college doesn't offer. You don't have to read any books to reach these educational milestones either. Nor do you have to write any term papers. No mid-terms. No finals. "What kind of majors and minors?" I hear you ask with jubilant anticipation. Consider these for starters:

Nightmare Solving—includes a variety of OJT (on-the-job-training) experiences, such as: owning a pet that bites the neighbors' children; renting an apartment from a lousy landlord; working for a boss who rates "–1" in fairness; and owing monthly payments a mere $33.50 more than your income.

Hair-Pulling Relationships—includes a wide variety of experiences with an accumulation of strangers and close associates, such as: living with a roommate who doesn't pay his or her half of the rent; working with a ranting and raving don't-wear-fur, save-the-seals activist; being married to a person who is exactly opposite from you in temperament; raising children who are never mistaken for angels.

Fix-it Management—includes a full study in the art of repairing broken machines, tools, vehicles, and other objects necessary in everyday life. Crawling under the hood of a steaming car in the middle lane of a five-lane freeway on a 103-degree day in August is the semester's highlight.

Body Politics—includes a full revelation of what it's like to gain twenty pounds within a year after graduation, start losing hair, and not have enough money to buy new clothes—all at once. This lifelong course gets more interesting with each passing decade.

Exhaustion—a very popular and commonly chosen major that includes a series of energy-draining occupations, chores, personal goals, and volunteer activities. Warning: the Surgeon General has declared that all middle-America taxpayers must choose this major.

Such is life. And that only scratches the surface. Wonderful and priceless as it is, life never cheats its participants out of sometimes painful lessons in growth and maturity. Living is its own best education, more valuable than rolling all the college majors and minors into one gargantuan degree.

Now for the guys I want you to meet. These guys lived truly unusual lives. I mean, really *lived.* Meet the Old Testament prophets. A much-overlooked bunch, this incredible crew of messengers make up a tremendous faculty for the University of Life. Some Bible teachers refer to them as "the Major and Minor Prophets." How that name came to be I'm not sure. A few of the prophets have longer books, which makes them "majors." And yet how on earth can we call the others "minors"? Are they less important? Certainly not.

I've never cared much for dividing the prophets into groups of "Big versus Little." As far as I'm concerned they are all major prophets. A little strange, but major. Yes, I said "strange." Each of these sixteen foreseers was called upon by God to perform outlandish acts and/or deliver shocking messages.

Crack open your Bible to Isaiah and work your way to the end of the Old Testament. You will read some bizarre stuff. You'll find Ezekiel cutting off his hair, separating it into three neat piles. He burns one pile, strikes the second with a sword, and throws the third to the wind. Later he silently sits naked in the streets, representing God's judgment. Today we would toss him in the loony bin, but God sent Ezekiel to deliver these bold visual messages.

Imagine Zechariah eating the great flying scroll instead of a tasty dinner roll. Observe while Jeremiah stands before King Zedekiah and tells him that the Babylonian army is going to take away his city. Look over Isaiah's shoulder as he peers down the annals of time to see that a "virgin will be with child and will give birth to a son, and will call him Immanuel" (Isa. 7:14). Spend a few moments with the lions in Daniel's den. Listen in when Amaziah the priest of Bethel lambastes Amos for his tough sermons, and the shepherd-turned-prophet answers, "Hey, I'm no prophet. I'm not even the son of a prophet. The reason I'm here is that God sent me."

What more could be said of Micah, who saw Bethlehem's star centuries before Jesus was born? Or of Jonah, who spent three nights in the worst motel this side of eternity? Whether it's Zephaniah or Habakkuk, you shouldn't miss the action. The names alone are worth checking out.

I'll be honest with you, though. The prophets aren't easy reading. If you stick with them for long, you probably will get sleepy. That's okay. Take a nap. Just keep coming back. These guys have stories you must read. And, if you look beneath the surface, you will find they have a message for today. Especially for graduates stepping out into the real world.

Hmmmm . . . Maybe that's why they call them the major and minor prophets—they speak to anyone entering the School of Life. Now there's a thought. Let's say we take a five-minute break and meet in Isaiah. Grab a Coke and some chips. The "son of Amoz" is stepping into the classroom.

Prophecies
of Excellence

Isaiah

To enjoy the things we ought and to hate the things we ought has the greatest bearing on excellence of character.

Aristotle

The doctor can bury his mistakes, but an architect can only advise his clients to plant vines.

Frank Lloyd Wright

1 Virtue

The Last Crusade

Whether you turn to the right or to the left, your ears will hear a voice behind you, saying, "This is the way; walk in it." [Isa. 30:21]

Indiana Jones—a name that is at once unusual and familiar. The mere mention of him conjures thoughts of excitement and adventure. Travel to faraway places. Experience the incredible. Survive the unbelievable. Defeat the intolerable. Find and recover the invaluable. And save the girl in the end. Indy is one of the all-time best examples of good triumphing over evil.

In a lot of ways, Indiana Jones teaches us about virtue. Simply put, virtue is moral excellence. Now I know Indy isn't always the perfect little trooper when it comes to high morals. I didn't say he was virtuous, especially not by God's definition. Still, we expect Indy to do the right thing in the end. We don't like our heroes to act like dirty birds.

One of the Old Testament prophets was a kind of Indiana Jones. His name was Isaiah. I doubt if he ever wore a leather hat or resorted to a bull whip to overcome his enemies. He didn't hunt for lost treasures or fall into pits of snakes. Isaiah lived a much tougher life than that. He spoke to a generation of people who barely could spell the word *virtue*. Yet he lived a truly virtuous life for them all to see and criticize. The Jews of his day stared at the prophet like a cow stares at a new gate. They just couldn't figure out why he was there.

Yet the old prophet's lectures live on for those of us who seek a degree in righteous living—a major for which you won't find many courses in a college catalog. So why not lend an ear? Join Professor Isaiah in Virtue 101. His first lesson might go something like this:

Virtue is about purity. Isaiah 52:11 records God's challenge for his people to come out of the smelly ruins of polluted living. "Purity" should not be viewed in a narrow sense, as an electric fence meant to corral those who might otherwise stumble into abusing their God-given sexuality. (You all know what I mean by that.) Rather, it should be seen as the highway to sexual freedom—the freedom to enjoy intimacy as it was meant to be. Virtue sounds the bell for purity. It says, "Where I lead, no one is ashamed to follow." Purity is plain, clean living. That's what virtue is about. Whoever is not pure cannot be virtuous.

Virtue is about innocence. God had a name for the masses who heard Isaiah's words. He called them "a people loaded with guilt" (Isa. 1:4). Not exactly a flattering description. Wherever they went and whatever they did, guilt followed along, weighing them down and poking them like a hard pebble in their shoes. It poked them in the morning; it poked them as they worked; it poked them when they rested. A constant reminder that they had done wrong.

Being "eaten up" with guilt is a dreadful experience. Ever been there? The disobeyed conscience trips over the gentle whispers of God and falls into the deep ravine of remorse. That's where God shouts into a great megaphone, and the echoes of his Spirit ripple across the wounded conscience. Too many times in my life he has needed his megaphone. And I'm here to tell you it takes a while before your ears stop ringing. God knows how to get our attention if he wants it. Unfortunately, when things get that far out of control, innocence has usually been lost, and the scars upon the healing soul endure for a lifetime. Better to be guarded by innocence than goaded by guilt.

Virtue is about honor. Isaiah 45:4 contains one of Scripture's smoothest phrases: "I summon you by name and bestow on you a title of honor." Graduation is a wonderful time of ceremony. The traditions, the awards, and the accolades all come together to make the event one of life's most memorable milestones. God has a graduation system of his own. He gives out degrees, too, so to speak. You might be glad to know he isn't looking for straight A's. Spiritual GPA isn't his kick, but God *is* into honor. He applauds those who don't feel they have to step on others to rise above being little in life. That is why the weakest are often the most honorable in God's eyes. They haven't been splattered with the muddy water of "me"-thinking. God takes special note of these people. The world may not recognize them, but God does. He calls them the "pure in heart" (Matt. 5:8). Their reward? They will see God.

It's been said that we never know the worth of pure water till the well runs dry. If that's true, we certainly should be starting to understand the value of virtue. Disease, divorce, and drug abuse—the killer *D*s—have fallen on us like acid rain. Our society has become disfigured because of them. Purity is fading, as are innocence and honor.

The time has come for a great crusade. Somebody call Indiana Jones. We've got a digging expedition to start, a search for a long-lost treasure. I doubt we'll be chased by Nazis, and we won't jump from airplanes or other adventurous stuff like that. But we will uncover one of God's rarest jewels: virtue. On the other hand, grab the white pages and phone for Isaiah instead. Do you suppose his last name was Jones?

2 Adaptability

Barefoot in the Park

You were wearied by all your ways, but you would not say, "It is hopeless." You found renewal of your strength, and so you did not faint. [Isa. 57:10]

I think Thomas has received too much bad press. You know who I'm talking about, don't you? Doubting Thomas. He was the disciple who had to see and touch the actual nail marks and put his hand into the very wounded side of Jesus before he would accept the resurrection. Thomas may have been unfairly branded all these years.

Was his problem really doubt? Or was he just having a hard time adapting to a world turned upside down?

Thomas probably would have been a terrific computer scientist. He liked having everything precisely figured out. I don't believe he doubted the Lord's ability to rise from the dead as much as he simply wanted proof. Thomas was not about to be hoodwinked.

My guess is that Thomas stayed a half-step off pace most of the time. He needed to see that every detail of a plan was going to work out before he could comfortably settle into a new routine. He was a no-risk kind of guy. Thomas might have been the first to say, "Let's get all our ducks in a row." Unfortunately for all the Tidy Thomases of the world, life is often unpredictable. Life, in fact, is very full of surprises.

Adapting to rapid changes in the world around you—to unexpected and unexplained events, and to life's typical ups and downs—takes some mastering. Most of us are a lot like Thomas. We don't care much for disruptions of our neatly organized schedules. However, since things rarely go as planned, learning to adapt is definitely one of life's majors.

We want daily living to go off without a hitch. We have this ideal of how things should be, and when they don't turn out that way we become frustrated, angry, or bitter. Some people might go so far as to manipulate a situation to control the outcome. Of course, you'd never do such a thing. Right?

Jacob, on the other hand, was as fine a manipulator as you'll ever meet. Genesis 27 tells how his mother, Rebekah, put goatskins on his soft hands to make him feel hairy like his twin brother, Esau. Why? To trick old Isaac into giving Jake the blessing due Esau as the firstborn son. Rebekah and Jacob didn't trust God to work out a perfect plan. They had to work out one for him. There are those who fight tough situations by carefully calculating everything (like Thomas), and there are some who do it by smoothly manipulating others (like Jacob).

The real solution is to adapt. As Isaiah suggests in the verse that tops this chapter, you must find a "renewal of your strength." Adapting calls for at least three qualities:

Tolerance. Some folks are too easily irritated by circumstances, which is evidenced by an attitude that says, "Don't tell me what to do, where to stay, what to wear, or how to act." Adapting is a hard trait for these types to master. Take Cain, for instance. He couldn't tolerate Abel's success. Abel was a good guy, but that didn't matter. Brother or no brother, Cain just couldn't abide competition. So human(un)kind recorded its first homicide. All because Cain couldn't accept Abel's apparently favored relationship with God. Impatient people almost always choke on adaptability.

Adjustment. This might mean change. I won't say too much about change here, because another chapter in this book takes a closer look at that subject. Make a note, however, that one of the keys to accepting change is time. Settling into a new church, a new job, a new home, or a new career path takes some getting used to. Give it time. You can adjust. Be careful not to force matters into *your* way of thinking. Let God work. Oscar Wilde said: "People are never so trivial as when they take themselves very seriously." Sometimes we should put aside all that is frantic and take time to walk barefoot in the park. Let someone else wear the Junior God merit badge.

Restraint. To give new situations time, you must sit still for at least a little while. This means holding yourself back from fighting difficult circumstances. When you'd rather run, you must simply watch and wait; when you'd rather have a fit, you must keep your spirit quiet. This is the hardest part of adaptability for me. I like to race ahead and figure out everything for God. You know, to save him some time. Kind of like a kid who runs up and down the grocery aisles. Mom already has a list, but the kid thinks this running-around jazz is pretty cool. Finally, Mom plops the youngster into the grocery basket. Now comes *mandatory* adapting. Unfortunately, sometimes God has to put us in the grocery basket, so to speak.

If Thomas and Jacob had studied under the tutelage of Professor Isaiah, I'm sure he would have given them his famous "Renewing Your Strength" lecture. He would have told them all about how to live in an unpredictable world. Even how to adapt without using calculators and goatskins.

3 Greatness

Where Eagles Dare

*You will go out in joy and be led forth in peace; the
mountains and hills will burst into song before you,
and all the trees of the field will clap their hands.*
[Isa. 55:12]

Denis Waitley tells a wonderful story in his book
Seeds of Greatness about how as a young boy he asked his
grandmother, in the dark days of World War II, whether
America would be taken over by the Japanese. His grandmother went to her room and brought back a handwritten
copy of a speech she had seen posted at her office. The

speech, which had been broadcast on the radio, was given by Madame Chiang Kai-shek, the First Lady and co-leader of the Chinese people in their struggle against the Japanese armies during the war. Grandma read these parts of the speech to Denis:

If the past has taught us anything it is that every cause brings its effect, every action has a consequence. We Chinese have a saying: "If a man plants melons he will reap melons; if he sows beans, he will reap beans." And this is true of everyone's life; good begets good, and evil leads to evil.

True enough, the sun shines on the saint and the sinner alike, and too often it seems that the wicked prosper. But we can say with certainty that, with the individual as with the nation, the flourishing of the wicked is an illusion, for, unceasingly, life keeps books on us all.

In the end, we are all the sum total of our actions. Character cannot be counterfeited, nor can it be put on and cast off as if it were a garment to meet the whim of the moment. Like the markings on wood which are ingrained in the very heart of the tree, character requires time and nurturing for growth and development.

Thus also, day by day, we write our own destiny; for inexorably . . . we become what we do.

When Denis's grandmother finished reading, she laid down her glasses and went into the kitchen to warm up a piece of rhubarb pie. (Yuk! Rhubarb has never been one of my favorites.) The response to her grandson's question was a bit strange, don't you think? Yet it was full of wisdom.

Madame Chiang Kai-shek touched on some key points about greatness. No, not fame, not fortune. Maybe not the

26

kind of thing that gets your name in the paper. Instead, she was really talking about the essentials of what Christians call victorious living. What are they?

A sense of accountability. James says, "Confess your sins to each other and pray for each other so that you may be healed" (James 5:16). Confession is tough; we hate to admit we're not perfect. Maybe that's what led the Catholics centuries ago to begin using little booths, known as confessionals, to give sinners privacy as they talked to the priest. It's hard for me to imagine James sitting in a confessional talking to the apostle Paul, but I'm sure he relied on other Christians for support and encouragement.

The whole concept of being accountable carries the idea of facing up to who we are, which includes taking personal responsibility for our own "destiny" as it relates to God's purposes for the universe. That's why our ultimate accountability is to God. Day by day he keeps tabs on us. What did he see in you today? That you spent time with him? That you cared only for what made you happy? That you made a difference in the world around you? What does today's record have to say about you?

A strategy for achievement. The law of sowing and reaping is as old as time. God taught it over and over in the Bible. Galatians 6:7 tells us plainly that "a man reaps what he sows." That's pretty easy to understand, isn't it? You can't plant corn and expect to harvest apples. You can't plant laziness and reap success. You can't plant hate and reap love. You can't plant bitterness and reap happiness. You can't plant trickery and reap honesty. The point is: To harvest true greatness, you must first scatter the right seeds. What are you going to sow in the ground of life? Like it or not, every day you're planting something. And you will have a harvest sooner or later. If you want to reap something desirable, study your seeds very carefully.

A commitment to abide. This was the Chinese First Lady's point when she said, "Character requires time and nurturing for growth and development." Great people hang tough. They give God time to work in their lives. Character, that inner who-you-really-are, doesn't take shape overnight. Not even in a year, or two years. This is why Jesus constantly stressed to his disciples, "Remain in me, and I will remain in you" (John 15:4). If you let God raise you as an eagle, you will not flap around like a baby sparrow.

In the last days before his crucifixion, Jesus talked with his disciples about greatness. He told them the startling truth that "whoever wants to become great among you must be your servant, and whoever wants to be first must be slave of all" (Mark 10:43–44). How do you like that? Strange plan for superstardom, wouldn't you say? Aspiring to true greatness is to crave being the servant of others. Grandma was saying, "Neither great individuals, nor great nations, are ever truly overcome by those with lesser character." (Fortunately I don't think that means we all have to eat rhubarb pie.)

4 Passages

Fantastic Voyage

. . . in quietness and trust is your strength. . . . [Isa. 30:15]

Even youths grow tired and weary, and young men stumble and fall. [Isa. 40:30]

Peter: Wendy, come with me.

Wendy: Oh, dear, I mustn't. Think of mother. Besides, I can't fly.

Peter: I'll teach you.

Wendy: How lovely to fly.

Peter: Wendy, when you are sleeping in your silly bed you might be flying about with me saying funny things to the stars. Wendy, how we should all respect you.

J. M. Barrie's ageless play about the rites of passage from childhood to adulthood is a story most of us grew up with. It is the tale of how a young boy afraid of growing up convinces a girl to join him on a journey of childhood fantasy on the eve of her maturity. So Peter Pan takes Wendy with him to Never-Never Land and the home of the legion of lost boys.

Many graduates can probably relate to Wendy, who has one foot in the playpen and another in the world of grown-ups. "The Wendy Dilemma" is a combination of feelings and struggles experienced by young adults who are leaving behind their childhood forever. And graduation is one symbol of that passage.

Trite as it may sound, you are entering the time of life when it is said that people must "find themselves." While you may think you know yourself very well, I expect the revelation you experience in the next few years will blow into pieces what you thought you knew. What makes "you" you? What do you want in life? What will be your goals and values? Will you be caught up in politics? Will you be involved in your community? These and a number of other questions will spring up and need to be answered by you during this time of transition.

Isaiah understood youth. References to youth are scattered throughout his message to the children of Israel. You know, I really can envision Isaiah teaching in a college classroom. I can hear him encouraging young women and men to live virtuous lives, to adapt to tough circumstances, to achieve greatness, and to ease out of the cocoon of adolescence into adulthood.

Read once more the verses that top this chapter. Do you have a feel for what Isaiah might say about your passage into adulthood? I think he would point out at least three factors faced by all young adults:

Confusion. This is an obvious aspect of the Wendy Dilemma. One day you might feel quite in control of your life, the next you might feel the familiar anxieties of your not-long-gone teenage years. Learning to be independent is a bag of mixed emotions. Understanding yourself is a noble and commendable goal, but don't be duped by the forces of the underworld. You don't have to leave everything behind to find the true you. Don't get me wrong; self-discovery is important. But that doesn't mean you have to let confusion overwhelm you into overhauling yourself completely. Accept the confusion. Let it teach you. Explore. But don't get confused about being confused, or you'll *really* be confused.

Power surge. It is an immutable law of kite flying that the one holding the string is in charge. As you begin to take possession of your life, of your future, expect some rough moments. After having lived for years under the leadership of your parents, you might find that being alone and in charge of your own choices can bring a major power rush. You quickly realize that when someone else writes your script, you're not living; you're just playing a part. So it feels good to call your own shots. Interesting days are these—days of believing you can change the world. But take care not to paint yourself into a corner during power surges. Life basically breaks down into three categories: (1) things that matter, (2) things that are of minor importance, and (3) things that added together still don't amount to anything. It's easy to get the categories mixed up. Isaiah might say, "Let quietness and trust be your strength, lest you stumble and fall."

Conflict. Whatever you do, offer ample compassion, understanding, and forgiveness to your parents during this passage. This is new stuff for them, too. It will take time for them to look past your childhood and see you as an adult handling the struggles of life's fantastic voyage. You are becoming their equal. This can be a hard adjustment for them, so you may have to emphasize to them that you have taken control of your own decisions. And yet, don't make them think you've lost respect for their opinions. Mark what Isaiah says: "Even youths grow tired and weary." You may need your parents' help someday soon. It is easier to lay a bridge of communication than to tear down a wall of silence.

How lovely it is to fly solo to unknown destinations! (But do work on a flight plan.)

Prophecies
of Challenge

*Jeremiah and
Lamentations*

*A prophet broke fresh ground—
because, and only because, he had
courage to go ahead without asking
whether others were following or
understood.*

Dag Hammarskjöld

*Your vision will become clear only
when you can look into your own
heart. Who looks outside dreams;
who looks inside awakens.*

Carl Jung

5 Criticism

The Lonely Guy

LORD, *you have heard their insults, all their plots against me—what my enemies whisper and mutter against me all day long. Look at them! Sitting or standing, they mock me in their songs.* [Lam. 3:61–63]

Leo Buscaglia, a professor of education at the University of Southern California, is known all over the world through the many translations of his best-selling books. In his terrific work *Bus 9 to Paradise,* Buscaglia recalls a cherished lesson from his childhood: "Papa used to tell me 'Felice, it costs nothing to be nice,' and after

35

waiting for the wisdom of that to settle in my mind, he would always follow with, 'And you get so much in return.'"

This reminds me of the story recorded several years ago at Harvard University when Dr. Robert Rosenthal conducted an interesting study involving three groups of students and three groups of rats. He told the first group of students that they would be working with "genius" rats. He said these rodents had been bred for intelligence, would eat tons of cheese, and would make it to the end of the maze in nothing flat.

Rosenthal told the second group that they would receive "average" rats as subjects. Not too dumb. Not too smart. Just average. They would eat some cheese and eventually make it to the end of the maze, but more slowly than the super-rats. The students were reminded not to expect too much from these little rascals of mediocre ability.

You've probably guessed that the third group of students was stuck with the "idiot" rats. This group was warned not to expect anything from their subjects. These rats are low performers, they were told. "You may not even need to give them cheese. They won't understand what you're trying to make them do. If one of them makes it to the end of the maze, it'll be a miracle," the professor said.

For six weeks, the students performed their experiments very carefully. Sure enough, the "genius" rats set all kinds of speed records in maze travel. The "average" rats were, well, average. And the "idiot" rats lived up (or should I say "down") to their billing, too. They had serious learning problems, and when one found his way to the end of the maze it was obviously by accident.

Here's the interesting part: There were no genius rats or idiot rats. All the subjects were plain old rats out of the same litter. The rats performed differently because they were treated differently. Obviously, each of the student

36

groups had formed opinions about their rats and passed on those attitudes of prejudgment to their furry friends. The experiment drove home this powerful truth: The way we are treated affects our behavior.

There is no shortage in this life of unsolicited opinions, criticism, and advice. You will not always receive the kind of treatment you think you deserve. Don't feel alone. Step into the classroom of Dr. Jeremiah, man of lament. He certainly took his share of barbs from people of less integrity than himself. And he made no bones about how much it hurt:

> They said, "Come, let's make plans against Jeremiah; for the teaching of the law by the priest will not be lost, nor will counsel from the wise, nor the word from the prophets. So come, let's attack him with our tongues and pay no attention to anything he says."
> Listen to me, O Lord; hear what my accusers are saying! [Jer. 18:18–19]

Someone once said, "Honest criticism is hard to take, particularly from a relative, a friend, an acquaintance, or a stranger." How aptly put. Let's face it—none of us likes to be criticized. None of us wants to be treated like an incompetent. Chances are, you can remember a recent incident when someone's faultfinding really got under your skin. Maybe it was an arrow of truth that found its way home. And yet, painful as it was, didn't you do your best to ignore how on-target the words were?

We each have at least one "Achilles' heel," a weakness, insecurity, or vulnerability that trips us up. Funny thing is, most of us will do almost anything to conceal our weak spots. We apparently figure people will think we're perfect as long as we have no flaws showing. Maybe we hide our Achilles' heel to avoid painful rejection by those who didn't have a father like Leo Buscaglia's. Either way can lead to loneliness.

The term *Achilles' heel* comes from the Greek myth of the great hero-warrior Achilles. According to legend, when Achilles' mother dipped him in the River Styx to make him invulnerable, the water touched every part except the heel by which she held him. That one unprotected spot was both proof of his being human and his potential downfall. Rather than accepting his vulnerability and learning from it, Achilles defiantly sought to prove he was invincible. He repeatedly exposed himself to attack, winning several battles before his bitter rival Paris shot a fatal arrow into his heel.

It isn't a big deal that you have at least one Achilles' heel. To be human is to have weaknesses. It does turn messy, however, if you let yourself get trapped into trying to cover up your vulnerable spots. True, criticism hurts. And, to be sure, there are some characters in life who seem to find enjoyment in exploiting the insecurities of others. Still, you must not let their insults con you into the Achilles complex—that is, being a loner because you think you must appear perfect in order to find acceptance. No snare is more constricting, no hoop is harder to jump through, than this one.

Since criticism is a hard reality of life, try your hand at majoring in managing it. Here are a few suggestions to get you started, but I'm sure you'll add your own ideas to the list:

Be a constructive critic yourself. Unless you're not a member of the human race, you find occasion to criticize others. We all do. We don't accept it well, but we're pretty good at handing it out. But remember the rats. How you treat people will affect how they respond. Nothing begets appreciation like appreciation. *If* you're sure you're seeing things correctly, practice using the same brand of helpful criticism you hope to receive from others. In other words, never go for the Achilles' heel!

Give a dozen compliments for every criticism. It's easier to remember the bad stuff. So you have to say more good stuff to offset it. People will respect your desire to be fair. In return, they will be fair with you.

Gentleness always crushes hostility. Nothing turns away anger like a gentle answer (Prov. 15:1). A super-criticizer usually has a need to be loved. Let your guard down. Maybe you'll end up friends. Leo's dad is so right: "It costs nothing to be nice." There is, however, a Paris waiting to zap everyone who tries to be invincible.

Don't choose a lonesome road. There may be a Paris waiting to zap every Achilles who tries to prove he's invincible, but hiding out is not the solution. Many a "lonely guy" has sealed his own fate by trying to run away from the possibility of rejection. Instead, accept the challenge. As Leo's dad said, "You get so much in return." So don't shy away from human contacts.

6 Impossibility

Superman

Ah, Sovereign LORD, you have made the heavens and the earth by your great power and outstretched arm. Nothing is too hard for you. [Jer. 32:17]

Here's a fine cliché: God is the God of miracles. Here is another: God is the Lord of the impossible. Sound stale? I guarantee you those words will be fresher than a sunlit spring day when you get into an impossible situation. You'll gasp for them like oxygen. They are as revitalizing as food and sleep. Anytime you hear that God can perform the unbelievable, you'll crack a smile of hope.

40

Many a game is won by an "impossible" field goal in the final second.

> Got any rivers you think are uncrossable;
> Got any mountains you can't tunnel through?
> God specializes in things tho't impossible;
> He does the things others cannot do.

I love the verse in Jeremiah that tops our chapter. When he says "nothing is too hard for you," he is using the strongest emphatic in the language. He's saying, "No, nothing, absolutely nothing for you, Lord, is too tough to handle." What we consider impossible, God considers less than a trifle. God sees our weaknesses. He sees that we are frail, that we are but specks of dust. Still, because we matter to him, God takes pity on our impossible situations.

One thing is clear in Scripture: God loves to work when no human solution can be found. When all is lost, when all seems hopeless, God takes over. Too often the reason we need God's last-minute intervention is that we've been trying to do it *our* way. We often delay calling on him until life gets really messy. As long as we still have a few ideas of our own, we consider God our last resort. Only when all our smart solutions are used up, and things seem out of control, are we prepared to listen. How like children we are! And yet, while it's true God works in the worst of times, we can't escape the consequences of waiting too long to ask him for help.

Hudson Taylor, the great missionary to China who saw many seemingly insurmountable circumstances during his years of ministry, used to say there are three phases in undertaking great tasks for God—impossible, difficult, done.

Many of us want to witness one of God's miracles, but we don't understand the nature of the miraculous. If you want to see a miracle, you must not fear incredible odds. The same Lord who took a few fishes and loaves and fed several thousand growling stomachs has a few fish left over for you. Is your mountain too high for him? Are your problems greater than God's wisdom and power? No? Well, good. Now, are they too big for you? Are they far beyond your strength? Not if you learn the three basic lessons of dealing with the impossible:

Letting go is half the battle. So you can't work it out. Admit it. You can't calculate a better way. Don't give up, but don't just hang on in desperation. Give *in* to God. Simply say, "Lord, I'm carrying something much too heavy for me. Will you take it?" This is not to say you should stop caring what happens. Of course you care. But the situation is now God's to do with as he pleases, when he pleases! You receive the relief of being rid of the weight and the joy of watching the miracle. And suddenly you'll feel strong.

Deliverance is God's work. When the children of Israel had their backs to the Red Sea and Pharaoh's army was bearing down on them, they must have wondered, "Why did we listen to this guy Moses? Now look at what he's gotten us into." Suddenly Moses shouted, "Stand still, and see the salvation of the Lord." Kersplash! The Red Sea opened under the blow of God's heavenly touch. Delivered!

This reminds me of the wonderful poem by Annie Johnson Flint:

> Have you come to the Red Sea place in your life,
> Where in spite of all you can do,
> There is no way out, there is no way back,
> There is no other way but through?
> Then wait on the Lord with a trust serene
> Till the night of your fear is gone;

He will send the wind, He will heap the floods,
When He says to your soul "Go on."

And His hand will lead you through—clear through—
Ere the watery walls roll down,
No foe can reach you, no wave can touch,
No mightiest sea can drown;
The tossing billows may rear their crests,
Their foam at your feet may break,
But over their bed you shall walk dryshod
In the path that your Lord will make.

In the morning watch, 'neath the lifted cloud,
You shall see but the Lord alone,
When He leads you on from the place of the sea
To a land that you have not known;
And your fears shall pass as your foes have passed,
You shall no more be afraid;
You shall sing His praise in a better place,
A place that His hand has made.

God performs the miracle, and we have nothing to do with it. All the glory belongs to him, which leads us to the third critical lesson of impossibilities.

Remember the miracles. We humans have a way of forgetting. The Israelites enjoyed one miracle after another, but they seemed to learn very little about appreciation in the process. They expected practically one a day. Whether it was the Red Sea or the manna or water from the rock, God just couldn't do enough. The shorter your memory, the less likely you are to observe the Specialist at work. Incidentally, don't make the mistake of taking credit for the miracles. God has all sorts of ways of reminding you who did what, and who only watched. You might remember how Job was called to the hot seat for a barrage of holy questions, such as: "Where were you when I laid the earth's foundation? Tell me, if you understand. Who marked off its dimensions? Surely you know!" (Job 38:4–5).

"God is the God of miracles" is no meaningless cliché to those who have been in dire need of a miracle and received it—because they asked correctly.

7 Dreams

Heaven Can Wait

*Call to me and I will answer you and tell you great
and unsearchable things you do not know.* [Jer. 33:3]

Henry Ford, the originator of the assembly-line method of building cars, launched his first ad campaign with a terrific promise: "You can have any color automobile you want, as long as it's black." Those were the Model-T days when getting around was far more important than how snazzy you looked while getting there. Not so today. Color, shape, speed, and electronic gadgets are as necessary to automaking as tires and doors.

On another occasion Henry Ford offered a bit of wisdom that I've come back to many times. He said: "Think you can, or think you can't; either way you're right." He was talking about dreaming, goal setting. Ford was a big dreamer and a big doer. No wonder he was a big achiever.

Can you see how this chapter fits with chapter 6? An "Impossibility" is a challenge that cries for hope; "Dreams" are hopes that challenge. Consider this: If you truly believe in God's ability to do the impossible, you can't dream impossible dreams. Impossible for you, perhaps; but not impossible for God.

The great Walt Disney loved to tell the story of the boy who wanted so much to march in a circus parade. When the big-top show finally came to town, the band needed a trombonist. The boy signed up. He had barely marched a block when the sounds from his screaming instrument brought looks of disgust.

"Why didn't you tell me you couldn't play the trombone?" the bandleader asked.

The boy answered matter-of-factly, "How did I know? I never tried before."

He majored in what too many recent graduates are afraid to consider—daring to dream. If you're like me, you're tempted to skip over some possibilities in life because the chance for failure is high. Most of us want a sure thing. Unfortunately, though, with sure things you miss adventure. You also miss finding out if you were capable of something greater than you could imagine.

What the world really needs is dreamers—but dreamers with ladders. They not only set high goals, but they have a plan for reaching those goals. They are not like the man who prayed, "O God, spare me from the hell of seeing the great opportunities I missed because I lacked the faith to believe and begin." These dreamers climb. They want to go up, and they have a perfect way to get there.

What is your dream? Everybody has a dream. Big dreams, little dreams. What is yours? Maybe it immediately comes to you when you hear the question. Maybe it's buried deep within, and you keep it bottled up because somebody once shot it down when you shared it. For many years I held a certain dream in secrecy because I was afraid of what people would think or say. By the grace of God, I've overcome that fear. I hold on to my dream to someday write a screenplay that is made into a movie. Whether your dream is great or small, easy to share or quietly hidden, take a few moments to consider these nuggets on dreaming:

Fear of failure paralyzes. Why do we fear failure? Yeah, I know nobody likes to lose. Nobody likes to fail. Still, why do we fear it so much? Maybe it's because we hate being embarrassed, and our mind is programmed to think that failure makes us look foolish. So we run around trying to be perfect, tackling what seems easy and shunning any dream that carries too high a risk. When Moses was handpicked by God—you know, the burning-bush story of Exodus 3—he didn't want to go back to Egypt to rescue his people. He feared failure. Moses asked God to send Aaron along to help out. Fine, God sent Aaron to help timid Moses overcome his crippled attitude about failure. Funny thing, though, Moses didn't fail. That's the way it is most of the time. We fear failing so much that the terrific possibilities for success get lost in the shuffle. We're so sure we're holding a bad bunch of cards, we don't even notice we've been dealt four aces. Like Moses, we need a burning-bush experience, something to get us moving. Look around— then give your dreams a chance.

Painful memories immobilize. Old hurts, setbacks, and previous rejections can bring your dreams to a complete standstill. "How could she have done that to me? I'll never forgive the things she said." "Why did he treat me that way? I've never been so humiliated in my entire life. I'll never forget what he said." These are the ugly messages we repeat again and again in our minds when we let damaged emotions do our thinking. Our prophet, Jeremiah, experienced one painful setback after another. So overwhelming was his disappointment that he was nicknamed "the weeping prophet." Still, he never lost sight of what God called him to do. He seized his dream. He held on to the promise of "great and unsearchable things." Escape from yesterday's pain. Choose to forgive others' unkindness and your own past lapses. Let yourself dream again.

Positive thinking capitalizes. Hey, if God is for you, who can be against you? (Rom. 8:31). Come on, name somebody. You may be wondering, "But is God really for me?" Perhaps the better question is: "Are you for God?" If you are, what can possibly stop you from believing your dreams will come true? Think big. Remember: Big things happen to big thinkers; little things happen to the small-minded. "Think you can, or think you can't; either way you're right."

There are more colors than black. Choose one. Choose several—and all the optional add-ons as well!

Prophecies of Fire

Ezekiel

It was not by gentle sweetness and womanly self-abnegation that she brought order out of chaos in the Scutari Hospitals. . . . Beneath her cool and calm demeanor, there lurked fierce and passionate fires.

Lytton Strachey,
writing about Florence Nightingale

Life is no brief candle for me. It is a sort of splendid torch which I have got hold of for a moment, and I want to make it burn as brightly as I can before handing it on to future generations.

George Bernard Shaw

NO CHILDREN
ON THE TOYS

8 Change

A Man for All Seasons

*Rid yourselves of all the offenses you have commit-
ted, and get a new heart and a new spirit. . . .* [Ezek.
18:31]

The story is told of a little boy who went with his
mother to a large toy store. A big sign that hung in plain
sight said: "Children are not allowed to play with the toys
or on the toys." Ignoring the sign, the boy jumped up on a
rocking horse and started riding to his heart's content. His
mom said, "Come on, son, you've got to climb down from

the horse." The boy pushed her away despite her scolding. She tugged at him, but he held on to the horse for dear life.

A clerk soon approached the mother and boy and said, "Sorry, but the sign says 'No children on the toys.' But if your mother wants to buy it. . . ." The boy ignored the man as much as the sign, so the clerk called for the manager. He tried to lift the boy down, but the child's grip was firmer than ever.

The manager said, "Son, if everybody came and played on the toys like you, the toys would soon be broken down, and we could not sell them. Now it's time to get off the horse." But still the child wouldn't budge.

Finally, a rough-spoken, rugged-looking man who had been watching the whole charade strolled over casually and said, "Let me talk to him." He bent over and gently whispered something in the boy's ear. Immediately the child climbed off the toy horse and said, "Okay, Mama, it's time to go home."

Surprised by the man's effectiveness, the mother asked her son, "What did the man say to you?"

The boy answered, "He told me to get down off the horse or he'd break every bone in my body."

Strange methodology, but it worked. It reminds me of something one of my college professors used to say, "People don't always heed warnings, but they sure understand consequences." The little boy understood about consequences. Since he didn't care much for broken bones, he cleared out. Unfortunately, tough talk and hard circumstances are the only logic some folks listen to.

That's what the major and minor prophets are all about. In the midst of captivity, rebuilding, and judgment, God was changing the face and soul of a nation. As a people, Israel had grown fat and complacent. Their blubber was so thick they couldn't see that their souls were untied and drifting. Change had to come. Drastic change.

What a word—*change*. Basically it means "to turn one thing into another." This might happen in a flash; or it might require a gradual, painful chiseling away of tiny unwanted pieces. The flash method is popular with most humans but is usually less effective. The chisel technique is dreadful, but it has highly profitable long-term results. Yet something tells me you're not the chisel type. You want fast relief. Can't say that I blame you. I've been beneath the chisel a few times myself and consider it much worse than the dentist's drill. (And my dentist drills like he's running a jackhammer and enjoying it.)

If you read chapter 2 on "adaptability," you already know that adapting to change can be a tall challenge. But you know that change is essential to growth. Besides, it wards off boredom. If you stay the same, where will life's challenges come from? Ezekiel rocked a nation stuck in neutral. He pleaded with them to change. He talked of God's demand for "a new heart and a new spirit." And his words ring out to sluggish Christians today. It's time for a change.

Change is life. After fifteen years away from my hometown, I took a trip down memory lane with my kids. We visited the elementary school I attended, the ball fields where I played Little League, the junior high and high school where I endured my teen years, and the two houses where I grew up. Not much was the same. The school classrooms were switched around from at least two remodelings. The baseball diamonds aren't even used anymore—a new stadium replaced them. The houses and streets were completely different. Where broad expanses of grass once awaited our days of football and catching lightning bugs, there now stands a strip mall with a huge supermarket. "Old things are passed away; behold all things are become new" (2 Cor. 5:17 KJV). All those changes startled me at first. Then they made me feel old. Don't laugh. It will happen to you one day.

Change is necessary. Why we fight change, I don't know. Well, that's not true. I do know. We fight change because we like to be comfortable. Change stirs things up. This is actually what made Jesus so unpopular with the crowds. His ideas dumped the world on its ear. Just when folks thought they had the Lord figured out, he threw them a curve. Jesus was, and still is, in the business of changing lives. Recliners don't fit into his scheme of things. I mean, if you're thinking of resting on your spiritual laurels, Jesus has some major surprises in store for you. God uses change to unsettle us from mediocrity, to eventually make us better servants.

Change requires right timing. When Saul of Tarsus was transformed into Paul the apostle, it was because he was ripe for change. God's alarm clock buzzed, and the outcome simply overflowed. You can't rush God's timepiece. If you try to change before your time, you will be no different. It must be God who changes you. You can argue with him, try to rush him, and complain. Doesn't help. What's more, if you're truly interested in changing this mixed-up world, you must let God change *you* first. It can either be interesting, or a miserable tug-of-war.

I would expect a chisel if I were you. But if all goes well, nobody will have to break all the bones in your body.

⑨ Balance

The Razor's Edge

"You will fall in the open field, for I have spoken,"
declares the Sovereign LORD. [Ezek. 39:5]

I like the little poem "Love-Songs, at Once Tender and Informative." Poet Samuel Hoffenstein says a lot in a few simple lines:

> Your little hands,
> Your little feet,
> Your little mouth—
> Oh, God, how sweet!

Your little nose,
Your little ears,
Your eyes, that shed
Such little tears!

Your little voice,
So soft and kind;
Your little soul,
Your little mind!

Know anyone like that? I think it's safe to say this little ditty is about a rather shallow woman. Apparently she is a gorgeous little doll. What a beauty to behold! But what a dingbat to talk with. Problem? Personal imbalance. Forgive me for seeming to single out women. I promise I'm not sexist, and I know that both genders can be guilty of having "little minds."

The truth is, all of us are somewhat imbalanced. Not everyone is a mental lightweight or chooses to act like one. But there are other aspects of life to consider, such as personality (little emotions), preferences (little desires), perceptions (little insight), prejudices (little tolerance), and personal behavior (little sense).

My theology professor reminded us of a simple truth almost every time the class met. He would say: "Balance is the key to the Christian's life. It's not how much Scripture you know, or how dedicated you are, or how many souls you win to Christ. Anybody can develop a measure of skill at these things. One cannot become skillful, however, at living a life filled with joy and contentment. You either possess this level of peace or you don't. It's that simple. Such blessings are the direct result of balanced living. So balance is the key."

Ezekiel knew something of balance. I mean, look at the prophecy selected for this chapter: "You will fall in the open field." That takes some doing, don't you think? The context explains that no one can escape judgment. Yet isn't it true that all falls are the result of imbalance? Would you believe that Ezekiel used the word *fall* no less than forty times in his series of messages? I'd say his listeners had a real problem with balance. Perhaps we shouldn't be surprised at their clumsiness in open fields. Dr. Ezekiel seems the right candidate for helping all who would major in Tumble Control. What might he say if he were here today? Perhaps this:

Guard against being too dogmatic. Just as you'll see in the next chapter, you should never shy away from being passionate in your pursuit of righteousness. But be careful *how* you present your dearest beliefs to others. Your thinking may change through the years, so how will you explain your new outlook to everyone who heard your other-side-of-the-fence ranting? Take it from an expert in bullheadedness, dogmas often come back to bite. And they chase off people, too. As Reuel Howe said in *The Miracle of Dialogue:*

> Indeed, the need of individuals to be right is so great that they are willing to sacrifice themselves, their relationships, and even love for it. This need to be right is also one which produces hostility and cruelty, and causes people to say things that shut them off from communication with both God and man.

Know your own weaknesses. Don't be so oblivious to your shortcomings that others will have to point them out to you. Flaws aren't easily hidden. We kid ourselves if we think so. If you're the moody sort, be careful your moods don't toss you around like a traveler in a strong wind. If you're a "half-empty" kind of thinker, practice more at having a "half-full" attitude. Know your weaknesses well and you will not be so surprised when a criticizer takes aim. You'll be able to listen with an honest ear and know that your weakness may be even worse than the critic thinks. That's humility, which does wonders for your equilibrium.

Don't overstrengthen your strengths. When I was a junior in high school, I knew a guy on the summer crew of the Parks and Recreation Department whose left arm was about one-third larger around than his right. It looked pretty weird. He told me it happened because he was always working out more with his left arm than his right. Lopsidedness is bad for balance. Christians can get lopsided by majoring too much on their major. Perhaps you're a natural storyteller already. So why not practice at listening to others tell the stories? If you're an expert on the Gospels, try the minor prophets on for size. Keep your spiritual muscles equally strong.

Most of all, watch where you're going. Each of us is capable of falling in an open field. In the immortal words of Ogden Nash:

> Beneath this slab
> John Brown is stowed.
> He watched the ads,
> And not the road.

10 Passion

Some Like It Hot

I will give them an undivided heart and put a new spirit in them; I will remove from them their heart of stone and give them a heart of flesh. [Ezek. 11:19]

Passion is an elegant word. We do it injustice by limiting it to the bounds of sexuality, because passion means so much more than sultry love. The world uses the word to sell merchandise and to name cologne, but passion is another major you need to work on. (Yeah, sexual connotations aside). Here's part of what one dictionary records about the word:

pas•sion [fr. Latin *passus,* pp. of *pati* to suffer] **1.** The suffer-
ings of Christ between the night of the Last Supper and his
death **2.** Suffering **3.** Emotions as distinguished from reason—an intense, driving, or overmastering feeling **4.** Strong
liking for or devotion to some activity, object, or concept **5.**
Sexual desire.

Surprised? So was I. At least somewhat. I didn't expect to
see a reference to Jesus Christ in the dictionary listing for
"passion." I find it especially interesting that the definition
talks about Christ and about devotion. That's exactly how I
want to look at the word in this chapter.

A few years ago Major F. J. Harold Kushner, an army
medical officer, shared a number of fascinating stories in an
article published in *New York* magazine. Major Kushner was
a prisoner for five years during the Vietnam War. Here is the
story of one man who was kept in that POW camp:

> Among the prisoners in Kushner's POW camp was a tough
> young marine, 24 years old, who had already survived two
> years of prison-camp life in relatively good health. Part of the
> reason for this was that the camp commander had promised
> to release the man if he cooperated. Since this had been
> done before with others, the marine turned into a model
> POW and the leader of the camp's thought-reform group. As
> time passed he gradually realized that his captors had lied to
> him. When the full realization of this took hold he became a
> zombie. He refused to do all work, rejected all offers of food
> and encouragement, and simply lay on his cot sucking his
> thumb. In a matter of weeks he was dead.

What happened here? This man lost his passion for life.
The intense, driving desire to survive was gone. When the
passion for life dies, the will to live disappears and we col-
lapse helplessly. We need passion if we are to suck every
drop of living out of every moment. Without it, life is dull.
Each day melts into the next, and goals are lost in the strug-

gle to "get by." The joy of living is slowly smothered, like a fire deprived of oxygen. If balance is the key (see chap. 9), passion is the door it opens.

Oh, to feel like Frederick Buechner, who wrote in *A Room Called Remember:*

> As much in my fifties as in my forties, I feel much of the time like a child. I get excited about the kinds of things that excite a ten-year-old. The first snow of the year, for instance. The smell of breakfast. Buying things, especially books, which, like a child, it is less important for me to read than simply to have. Getting things in the mail. Going to the movies. Having somebody remember my name. Remembering somebody's name. Making a decent forehand in tennis. Being praised. Chocolate ice cream. And so on.

Such passion for life! Of course, I know you aren't fifty. Not even close. Neither am I, but I feel older than that some days. Back to the subject. Just listen to Freddie. He feels like a kid again, so full of energy and excitement. And the little things of life mean so much to him.

Ezekiel had tremendous passion for his calling. How eagerly he must have relayed God's message in the key verse for our chapter: "I will give them an undivided heart and put a new spirit in them; I will remove from them their heart of stone and give them a heart of flesh." If that isn't a testimonial about passion, nothing is. Ezekiel 24:18 records what I believe to be one of Scripture's most incredible insights into this prophet's blazing fervor: "So I spoke to the people in the morning, and in the evening my wife died. The next morning I did as I had been commanded." In the face of suffering Ezekiel found strength to carry on. He never lost his zest for life.

What about you? Do you face the future with an enthusiasm fit for someone whose whole life is waiting to be discovered? Have you considered where to direct your passions? Sure, love and romance rank real high on your passion meter. That's okay. God doesn't expect you to poke your eyes out and ignore the opposite sex. Still, I hope you'll unleash your intensity for spiritual causes, too, such as:

Kingdom passion. Ezekiel had it. That's why he was able to proclaim God's message the day after his wife's death. He was compelled to serve God. Ol' Zeke wasn't so wrapped up in this brief life we have on earth that he forgot to make contributions to his eternal 401(k). Passion for God's plan is the theme of Matthew 6:33. Those who "seek first his kingdom" have discovered a powerful reason for living. They have found Life *himself.*

People passion. If the joys and pains of others don't touch you, are you really alive? For years I have served as a counselor both inside the ministry and as an everyday Christian. I am still amazed that my minutes of listening mean so much to those who need a caring shoulder to lean on. Today I wept with a friend who shared that someone he loves is dying of AIDS. Then I came home to laugh with my two children, who tickled me on the neck for thirty minutes. How blessed are we to have the freedom to relish life with others. May God help us not to miss sharing the good times and the bad.

Wide-eyed passion. This is the ongoing passion to learn and grow. Life is awesome, and so are its lessons. Passionate people hunger to absorb more. They keep searching. Wide-eyed passion knows better than to think it has all the answers. This is one area where it's sometimes a good idea to "think like a child"—with wonderment!

Take a few moments to remind yourself of how good life is. Of how good freedom is. Of how good God is. Then open a Pepsi and raise a toast to Zeke and Fred.

Prophecies
of Inspiration

Daniel

*I have never accepted what many
people have kindly said, namely,
that I inspired the nation: It was the
nation and the race dwelling all
around the globe that had the lion
heart. I had the luck to be called
upon to give the roar.*

Winston Churchill

*Imagination is more important than
knowledge.*

Albert Einstein

11 Friendship

Places in the Heart

Then Daniel returned to his house and explained the matter to his friends Hananiah, Mishael and Azariah. He urged them to plead for mercy from the God of heaven concerning this mystery, so that he and his friends might not be executed with the rest of the wise men of Babylon. [Dan. 2:17–18]

Tell me what you think: Are friends a luxury or a necessity? Some people don't believe having friends is all that important. Like the girl who recently told me, "Having friends is not such a big deal, especially if you're close to your family. Friends can be a hassle. They want your time, and often they can't be trusted. Busy people don't have time for friends—not real friends, anyway." It sounded to me as if she had been burned a time or two, because her outlook seemed so cynical. And yet, every day there are people who die without ever having experienced a real friendship.

Friends are a necessity in my life. There have been times when my friends literally rescued me from disaster. In prayer and in my private moments of reflection, I call out their names with gratitude—Martin, Doug, Al, Jim, Stan, Johnny, Bret, Sam, Tony. These guys have encouraged me, counseled me, laughed with me, cried with me, prayed for me, and shared their lives with me. When I've needed them, they have always been there. Even when my family was not. These friends have provided me with strength when I had none, and an example of faith when believing seemed the impossible thing to do. They have defined my idea of friendship.

Have you ever wondered why you become friends with some people and not with others? Isn't it strange that an unexplainable bonding takes place between people to make them friends? I mean, a connection that just doesn't happen with mere acquaintances. It's as if a little trick of the mind and heart matches us up with some people but not with others.

Sometimes it's just destiny. As in the case of Daniel and his friends. Not only were Hananiah, Mishael, and Azariah (AKA Shadrach, Meshach, and Abednego) Daniel's buddies, but the fellows were also his confidants. Why had he bonded with these guys? Mainly because of the circumstances. (Of course, a lot of what we call "destiny" is God's doing.) During the Israelite captivity in Babylon, there weren't too many Jewish teenagers to hang around with. Nonetheless, Daniel picked winners for friends—guys who really loved God and wanted to obey him.

All of you should add Dr. Dan's understanding of friendship to your schedule of courses. If you were to earn an M.B.A. from Harvard's School of Business but learned nothing about choosing or being a friend, how good would the degree really be? Oh, sure, you might go far in the corporate world. Big job. Big salary. Big house. Nice car. Nice clothes. No friends. All career, no life. Sounds grim.

Daniel had people he could turn to in time of trouble, although friends are much more than that. Because he had pals, Daniel was never alone in the world. Emerson might have pointed to Dan's example when he penned his stunning essay "Of Friendship," in which he wrote: "We take care of our health, we make our roof tight and clothing sufficient, but who provides wisely that we should not be wanting in the best property of all—friends?"

What do you look for in a friend? What makes a true friend? In a recent poll, hundreds of people were asked that question. It's interesting to note that almost everyone expected a friend to have certain qualities. According to the poll, here are the top four traits people look for when choosing their friends:

Loyalty and trust. One young woman said, "A friend is someone you can tell about your cellulite problem and she won't blab it to other people." Besides keeping your secrets, friends should be buffers and boosters. Buffers cushion the negative experiences of life; boosters enhance the positive. Recently I went through the worst ordeal of my life. I wondered who I could turn to. With some embarrassment I called my friend Martin. Here's a guy who always beats me in golf, but Martin is a true friend. Thirty minutes after my call he left work to spend the afternoon encouraging me. I didn't expect that, but I certainly was grateful for it. Martin continued to be there for me through the next several weeks. That kind of loyalty is the core of friendship.

Generosity. Someone once said, "A friend in need is not a friend." I don't agree, but I get the message. People who take advantage of their friends by always being on-the-take give friendship a bad name. Yet true friends are openly generous. They know how to help out their pals, and they willingly make sacrifices. I've also heard it said, "Don't worry about loving your enemies, just concentrate on loving your friends." While Jesus wants us to love our enemies, some of us could also do a better job of loving our friends. Love means giving. Love is generous.

Acceptance. Perhaps the most common quality people look for in a friend is unconditional acceptance. As hundreds have said in one way or another, "A friend is someone who knows me and likes me anyway." None of us has so much love in our lives that we couldn't stand a little more. This doesn't mean we can treat friends however we please, figuring they'll love us anyway. I've known some people who manipulated and mistreated their friends. Those types usually end up friendless.

Honesty. Real friends tell you what you *need* to hear, not just what you *want* to hear. And, because you trust and respect them, you can bear the truth from them. When friendship reaches this level, it has steady legs that stand up under time and trouble.

Having friends is important, but perhaps being a friend is even more important. How good a friend are you? Do you have the kind of traits you look for in a friend? Would you choose *you* as a friend? The greater question is not "Do others have what you're looking for?" but "Do you have what others are looking for?"

Socrates said, "There is no possession more valuable than a good and faithful friend." Because I know that's true, I thank God for the Martins in this world.

12 Uniqueness

In the Heat of the Night

Then Daniel answered the king, "You may keep your gifts for yourself and give your rewards to someone else. Nevertheless, I will read the writing for the king and tell him what it means." [Dan. 5:17]

The night before last I was carrying out the garbage at dusk when a young man came strolling across my lawn. A guy from GreenPeace. Have you heard of GreenPeace? It's a big group of environmentalists bent on saving the planet. I like some of their ideas.

Anyway, this guy was really nice. His name was Adam. Perfect name for an environmentalist. It means something like "man of red earth." I liked Adam's unique style. He is definitely his own person. Dressed in a khaki shirt, blue jeans, and army boots, with his hair pulled back in a pony-tail, Adam was "evangelizing" our neighborhood with GreenPeace magazines and taking donations. I didn't donate, but I did take a magazine. Pretty interesting stuff. Here's the fine print on the intro page:

> The cover of this magazine is made of paper we import from Sweden. We use it to make a point: Almost all paper in the United States and Canada is bleached with chlorine, creating dioxin-laden chlorinated pollution. This paper is bleached using an oxygen-based process, making it safer and cleaner. Using it is a small but significant step toward our ultimate goal: the exclusive use of post-consumer recycled paper that, when necessary for high quality, is bleached using a non-polluting technology. The paper inside this magazine is printed on recycled paper.

GreenPeace is a group of rare individuals. I don't agree with everything they believe in, but I respect their tenacity of spirit. It represents the kind of bold originality I like to see in people.

Know what? A similar spirit abides within you, waiting to be put into action. No, I'm not talking environmentalism. What I mean is that there's only one you! (What a comforting thought for the rest of us. Just kidding!) Really, you're one of a kind. That's a fantastic truth. God made you for a particular purpose, and no one else can fill your space in life. We need you in this world. You are the only one who can do things the way you do them and say things the way you say them. Your distinctive insights cannot be duplicated, stolen, or imitated. You are unique—special in every way.

70

Expressing one's uniqueness draws attention. Folks have always been fascinated with out-of-the-ordinary people, places, and things. We grow weary of the same-old same-old. Take vacations, for instance. Would you prefer to stay home and work on your house, or visit a new place where you never have been? Or take performers. Why is Madonna such a smash hit? (Even though I don't admire her or her work.) Same reason any music star is—she's kind of eccentric, not afraid to be different. She doesn't let anyone tamper with her image of individuality. Millions of fans buy her records. Uniqueness pays off in show biz—and in real life, too.

All of the prophets were genuine articles who knew their own worth. Take Amos, for example. He was a fig-picker. He picked fruit from sycamore trees. This fruit is a lot like figs. Messy stuff. It stains your hands if you mash it. Imagine Amos at a job interview:

"What is your current occupation, Mr. Amos?"

"I pick figs."

"You are a farmer?"

"Yes, I've been tending sheep and picking figs for several years."

"Well, why do you think you're qualified to become a prophet?"

"Actually, I think tending sheep is excellent experience for leading people. And picking figs is very messy work, a lot like being a prophet."

"Interesting, but we have never hired a fig-picker for this position."

"I can understand your apprehension, but I am certain God wants me to do this."

Amos had a style all his own, as did Haggai and Nahum and Joel and all the other prophets. These men weren't bound by society's standards of personality or success.

No, sir. They were not conformists by any stretch of the imagination.

But Daniel is our "prophet of inspiration," and, like the others, he realized that God made him and then broke the mold. What is it that separated Daniel from the run-of-the-mill crowd? What made him so unusual in a day when people were preoccupied with uniformity? I believe at least four characteristics set young Dan apart from the rest—traits we would do well to emulate.

He was comfortable being himself. Daniel was kidnapped into a culture the very opposite of his own. The king saw to it that Daniel received secular training from the finest teachers and was given a relatively luxurious life in the palace. Yet Daniel didn't lose his Jewish heritage and personal identity. He wasn't worried about whether the Babylonians would like him or whether he fit with the "in" crowd. Daniel was Daniel and nobody was going to change that. This example should inspire any college-bound student or other young adult who will fall under the pressure of overconformity.

He lived by his own values. The bad guys in the "Lions' Den" story hated watching Daniel pray. He knew that. Still, he threw open the shutters in their plain sight and prayed anyway. Daniel placed high value on prayer. He wouldn't give it up, no matter how much pressure the hoodlums put on him. Early in the Book of Daniel we also read that he refused to eat food from the king's table, because it had been first offered to idols. Daniel knew what he believed, and he remained unshaken in his faith.

He wasn't afraid to trust God. When being obedient to God threatened Daniel's safety, he obeyed just the same. He wasn't chicken-hearted. Tough times make tough people. The young prophet believed that God would take care of him. He didn't sacrifice permanent truths on the altar of the immediate. So a potentially terrifying event in the lions' den turned into a yawning match. The result? Daniel's unique faith and obedience brought unbelievers to faith in his God.

He lived on a higher plane. Daniel didn't stoop to the tactics and morals of the heathen who surrounded him. He existed a cut above the rest. Not that it was easy. Sure, he was bright and enterprising, but circumstances were not altogether kind to the teenager. He lost his family when he was carried into captivity. What a terrible upheaval he experienced! In the face of all this, Daniel kept his composure and walked with God. Unique indeed!

I pressed the electric garage-door buttons and watched Adam head to the neighbor's house. Though his Green-Peace ideology and personal appearance were kind of a throwback to the '60s, I admired him. He had the courage to be himself, and he wasn't ashamed. Too bad more Christians don't have the dedication of this young man. If God can use a displaced person like Daniel or a fig-picker like Amos, he can use you. Just let him.

JUST REMEMBER, YOUR FINEST HOUR IS APPROACHING.

13 Courage

Chariots of Fire

> *If we are thrown into the blazing furnace, the God we serve is able to save us from it, and he will rescue us from your hand, O king. But even if he does not, we want you to know, O king, that we will not serve your gods or worship the image of gold you have set up.*
> [Dan. 3:17–18]

Barely one month after Winston Churchill promised the British people that their "finest hour" was approaching, he told the nation on July 14, 1940:

And now it has come to us to stand in the breach and face the worst the tyrant's might and enmity can do. . . . We are fighting by ourselves alone . . . but we are not fighting for ourselves alone. . . . We await undismayed the impending assault. Perhaps it will come next week. Perhaps it will never come. We must show ourselves equally capable of meeting a sudden violent shock, or what is perhaps a harder test, a prolonged vigil.

Some time later, when Great Britain was being battered by enemy bombs day and night, several of its frightened leaders began plotting the evacuation of the island. Churchill answered, "Wars are not won by evacuation." This great leader made many inspiring statements, but he is probably best characterized by what some consider his most memorable words: "Never give in! Never give in! Never, never, never, never—in nothing great or small, large or petty,—never give in except to convictions of honor and good sense!" It was the unyielding determination of this man that gave him the courage to speak such daring words of motivation.

Daniel's buddies Shadrach, Meshach, and Abednego were forged of similar iron. They had "the right stuff." Bear in mind, too, that they were just youngsters when they became administrators in idolatrous Babylon. Having been hauled off in the captivity of Israel, they were trained by King Nebuchadnezzar to become the finest leaders in all the land. He made sure they were polished, professional, and poised—straight off the pages of Babylon's *Gentleman's Quarterly*. One thing he could not affect was their hearts. Exercising the full spunk of their late adolescence, these three fireballs for God (no pun intended) became a living testimonial to courage.

"Go ahead and toss us in the furnace," they challenged the pagan king. "God can handle flames far better than you can handle God. We're not about to disobey him by kneeling to your dinky idol" (an Earles paraphrase).

Nebbie had little choice. He couldn't let these whippersnappers show him up in front of the entire kingdom. "Set the oven on extra hot," was his command. "Make it seven times hotter than ever before."

I'm not sure what this was supposed to accomplish. After all, fire is fire. A forest fire is bigger than a bonfire, but it isn't too much hotter; either would be quite sufficient to end a human life. A matter to consider, though, is God's delight in having the fire's heat intensified to the nth degree. This was not a dry sauna. Men didn't drop in for a morning sweat willingly. The king had himself a real death machine here. God likes such odds.

The fire was so outrageously hot that it killed the soldiers who threw the shackled lads into the furnace. The Hebrew boys? Well, they ran around freely in the flames with a fourth figure, described by the amazed observers as "a son of the gods" (v. 25). They were burnished with courage. In the end, even the king praised their God.

Take a few seconds to consider why God inspired Daniel to record this event as part of his prophecy. I'm sure he didn't do it just to amaze us, although it certainly is a fantastic story. So why did Daniel include it? I believe one undeniable reason is that God wants you and me to have a bedrock of genuine spiritual courage. A well of strength to draw from. A foundation to build on. Maybe Churchill was inspired by these young heroes.

One of the greatest speeches given to an army is recorded in 2 Chronicles 32:7–8, where King Hezekiah of Judah is rallying his men to face Sennacherib, king of the invading Assyrians. Imagine Hezekiah, sitting atop his horse at the gates of Jerusalem and shouting his oratory to a throng of soldiers who are hanging on his every word. Desperately seeking encouragement, they listen carefully as their leader's words ring through the morning air. No doubt his rousing speech was followed by loud "Huzzahs!" Listen for yourself: "Be strong and courageous. Do not be afraid or discouraged because of the king of Assyria and the vast army with him. . . . With him is only the arm of flesh, but with us is the LORD our God to help us and to fight our battles."

Dear graduate, this is the meaning of courage. Yet talking about it is easier than laying all your tomorrows on it. Anyone can boast of courage, but only those who walk with a limp know what it is to have it. With a limp? Thought you might catch that. Yes, a limp.

A friend once told me, "I don't trust anyone who doesn't walk with a limp." He was speaking figuratively, of course. Remember Jacob from our chat in an earlier chapter? He walked with a limp as a result of a wrestling match he had with God alongside the Jabbok River. At a crucial point in his life, Jacob had to learn that it was God who controlled his destiny. (You can read about the encounter in Genesis 32.) Jacob met God "face to face" in human form and struggled with him for hours. Suddenly, when God was quite ready, he grabbed Jacob by the thigh and wrenched his hip. Jacob never walked normally again. He was permanently changed that night. His attitude was different. His outlook. His purpose. Even his name, for God renamed him "Israel." Jake was changed forever by his limp. Where he once was a trickster, he now was courageous because he knew that God was in control but was on his side.

You're probably too young to have a limp just yet. Don't worry. It might come sooner than you think. Tough days could be around the corner for you, bringing a challenging situation to test your mettle. In that hour you might feel totally abandoned, as if God has forgotten your name. Energy and confidence will drain out of you like lake waters through a broken dam. You will feel empty. Then

God will see if you are ready to major in courage. Words like these won't be simple platitudes in that day.

What will happen? That depends on you. If you let him, the Spirit of God will show you who you really are—one of his own special team. God's presence and his love will become very real to you. Then, spiritually speaking, you will feel your hip socket and know you'll have a permanent limp. Because you will know who caused that limp—and why—your greater mission in life will become clear, and you will not be afraid.

I'm hoping this will happen for you. Not that I wish you to be hurt. But I believe that those who never endure struggles learn little about courage. They will quit later in life, because they will think that wars *are* won by evacuation. And the fire will consume them.

Prophecies
of Outlook

Obadiah and Joel

*No one ever would have crossed the
ocean if he could have gotten off the
ship in the storm.*
                              Charles Kettering

*If having a good time were all there
is to life, monkeys have mankind out-
distanced completely—both in amusing others and in being amused.*
                              Harry Banks

14 Empathy

Silence of the Lambs

You should not march through the gates of my people in the day of their disaster, nor look down on them in their calamity in the day of their disaster, nor seize their wealth in the day of their disaster.
[Obad. 13]

One dictionary defines empathy as "the capacity to participate in the ideas and feelings of another." You probably need to stop and mull that over for a second. Empathy is heavy stuff. It is a marvelous trait that allows us to step outside of ourselves and try to understand another person from within. In some cases no words are necessary. Feelings are automatically shared even when we don't have the ability to describe them.

From one of Grimms' *Fairy Tales* comes a peppery illustration of just how important empathy (or lack of it) can be. Did you ever read "Grandfather's Corner," the story of an old man who lived with his son and his son's wife? The old papa was almost totally deaf and blind and had difficulty eating without spilling his food everywhere. Occasionally he would drop a bowl and break it. His son and daughter-in-law found this disgusting and made him eat in a corner behind the stove. They gave him a wooden bowl that he couldn't break. Nice folks.

One day the old man's little grandson was quietly working with some pieces of wood. When his dad asked what he was building, he replied, "I'm making a trough for you and mother to eat out of when I'm grown up." From that moment on, his grandfather was allowed to rejoin the family at the table, and no one ever said another word about his messy habits. The thought that "I, too, may suffer this fate" has inspired many people to search for empathy with others.

Young as you are, you can probably relate to the grandpa. Like little lambs full of fear, most of us seldom bleat a word when we need special attention and care. We suffer in silence, thinking that no one will understand (much less care) and afraid to share our pain with anyone else. I am often amazed at how many people in this world need love and encouragement. It's overwhelming. Hurt is everywhere. Not that life is a total downer, because it isn't. Life, in fact, is quite wonderful. Still, the difficulties can be huge, much bigger than we can handle alone. Then we wonder, "Does anyone understand what I'm going through?"

A prayer to be said
When the world has gotten you down,
And you feel rotten,
And you're too doggone tired to pray,
And you're in a big hurry,
And besides, you're mad at everybody
   Help!
Charles Swindoll

Boy, do I know that feeling! We all do. Empathy goes deeper than this, though. Empathy sighs with those who have lost their second wind. It cries with those who are all cried out. It prays with those who have lost faith in prayers of their own. Empathy never preaches; it just reaches out. It doesn't wait for a cry of "Help!" Empathy is the silk lining of love.

The words of the prophet Obadiah hint at empathy. He is saying, "Hey, have gentle respect for victims of calamity—even if they deserved what came to them." Christians can be a judgmental lot. Some believers are long on justice and short on mercy. They are technically right about sin's consequences, but practically wrong about how to minister to the sinner. All of us could stand a few credit hours in "Basic Empathy."

Special talents come in handy. A good friend of mine who now lives in South Carolina used to cheer me up by playing his guitar. Music really soothes my soul, and he made the most of his special talent when it came to my down days. He had a full repertoire of goofy songs and hot licks. Like David who played the harp for Saul, he'd rattle tunes out of that six-stringer that never failed to lift my spirit. Develop a style all your own in ministering encouragement to others. Wrap your special talent—whatever it is—in a warm blanket of humor. If a spoonful of sugar helps the medicine go down, a cupful of humor makes the empathy go 'round—in a most delightful way.

Humans can be hard to care for. If you don't know this already, you haven't lived long enough. Empathy is not as easy as saying, "Oh, things aren't going well? Here, let me feel your frustration." Some folks are downright impossible to comfort or even understand. Anne Tibble, describes them with these hilarious lines:

> Can you give me something for diarrhoea?
> I have a pain. Here.
> I have pains all over.
> I can't eat.
> I do not sleep.
> I think I have a temperature.
> I have caught a cold.
> I have been burnt by the sun.
> My skin is smarting.
> Have you nothing to soothe it?
> My nose is bleeding.
> I keep vomiting.
> I have been bitten by a dog.
> I think I have food poisoning.
> You are hurting me.
> I shall stay in bed.
> Bring me something to drink—please.
> Help!
> Fire!
> Thief!

Try empathizing with all that. If you find these complaining types easy to care for, you have earned a Ph.D. in empathy!

Jesus was and is an empathizer. (Check out Hebrews 4:15–16.) Although Jesus was the Son of God and without sin, when he was on earth as a man he faced the same kind of temptations and frustrating situations we all do. So Jesus feels our infirmities. He knows what we're going through. When no one else understands, he does. Read the Gospels and marvel at the way he caressed the wounded spirits of those who came to him. How rarely he spoke a harsh word. He ate in the homes of sinners, treating them like people worthy of love instead of criminals deserving of punishment. Jesus still rejoices with those who are rejoicing and comforts those who need comforting. He shows us how. Master teaching by the Professor Emeritus of shepherding.

Empathizers sometimes need empathy, too. All giving and no receiving makes Jack a burnt-out boy. Don't try to be superhuman. No one is strong enough to help others without ever needing some personal TLC. Don't be too proud to accept the love and kindness of others. Let others minister to you. It will be good for everyone. The giving will make them feel better, and the receiving will raise you up. The gift may be something as simple as time shared together. Receive it with gratitude. Put a smile on Anne Tibble's face.

15 Determination

Rocky V

They charge like warriors; they scale walls like soldiers. They all march in line, not swerving from their course. [Joel 2:7]

Vince Lombardi, the legendary coach of the Green Bay Packers who led his team to victory in the first two Super Bowls, is known for the immortal saying, "Winning isn't everything, it's the only thing." But people who actually knew Lombardi say he's been misquoted. In fact, they say that "winning by intimidation" was not really his spirit or his way. The transcripts have him saying something quite different: "Winning isn't everything—but the will to win is everything." The wording may seem only slightly different, but the meaning is changed completely.

The "will to win" cheerleads for determination. You know, we kiddingly say about this thing or that, "If I had a dollar for every time —— [fill in the blank], I'd be a millionaire." Believe me, if I had a dollar for every time I felt like quitting, I could afford lifetime worldwide cruises for all of us, with plenty of spending money in every port. But, thank God, I've never learned how to give up on God, life, or myself. I guess quitting scares me more than keeping on.

I'm reminded here of the words of the great heavyweight champion of decades ago, Jack Dempsey: "To win you have to be able to give and take hard punches." Giving hard punches is a lot more fun than taking them, of course. As James "Buster" Douglas said when asked how he became the first man to beat the awesome "Iron" Mike Tyson, "I hit him hard and often." Whatever the obstacle, whatever the project, delivering hard punches is what it takes to win a knockout. If you're the namby-pamby type, expect to get bruised a lot. Life is going to shove you around until you wise up and throw some sharp jabs of your own.

I'm not being a cynic. Life isn't mean and cruel, although sometimes it seems that way. I'm not suggesting that you walk around with a chip on your shoulder. If you do, somebody will gladly knock it off for you. Just add a little thickness to your skin and learn Professor Joel's balanced approach to determination.

You can't be beaten if you don't quit. What made Rocky so lovable? Apollo Creed knocked him down again and again, but he kept getting up. Almost everyone admires Rocky's stick-to-itiveness. He epitomizes what many of us want to have: enough determination to bounce back. Paul told the Ephesians that God is "able to do immeasurably more than all we ask or imagine" (Eph. 3:20). I think this was another way of phrasing what several of the Old Testament prophets had said. Work on a minor from Paul and Joel. Go ahead, imagine some terrific things you'd like to see accomplished in your life. Guess what? God can do more than that. But you've got to do your part.

God likes us to be tough-minded. He gives us enough strength for the day at hand. That's why we shouldn't waste any of it *worrying* about the future. Tomorrow's strength is for tomorrow. Some people are hold-outs for the "safe bet." They are waiting for life to fit their plans and won't jump into cold and unknown waters. Pardon me, but too many Christians just don't have any "guts." They have backbones of jelly. The tiniest setback spooks them into fear and defeat. Sure, Jesus wept. And he prayed earnestly. Sometimes he simply sat quietly while the world raged all about him. Yet Jesus could level the Pharisees with a couple of sentences; he could clear the temple with one pass through the courts. Jesus is our example of tender tough-mindedness. Now is the time for the fainthearted to stop complaining and deal with life's challenges head-on.

Your worst times can become your best times. In a hundred ways the prophets told the people of God this truth. They didn't hear it. Do you? Do you buy into it? You know, it's true we can be such babies. The apostle Paul once told the Corinthians to grow up and be courageous and strong (1 Cor. 16:13), a few short chapters after telling them to stop thinking like babies (1 Cor. 14:20). Ouch! Bet that hurt. We whine and worry a lot. Frequently we expect the worst and bring to pass our own pessimistic prediction. You might be wondering, "Well, then, how do the worst times become the best times?" The answer is simply this: Bad times have the potential of bringing out either the best or the worst in us. The choice is ours. An ancient

Greek philosopher named Heraclitus said, "Where there is no strife, there is decay: The mixture which is not shaken decomposes." Where does joy come from, anyway? Sure, from the Spirit of God, but that's not what I mean here. Under what circumstances does real joy spring alive? Only the good ones? Hardly. Of course, eating the fruit of good times tends to give us a rush of euphoria, but lasting joy swells out of knowing that God is bearing you up in the worst of times.

God has enough determination for both of you. God told Jeremiah, "Today I have made you a fortified city, an iron pillar and a bronze wall to stand against the whole land . . ." (Jer. 1:18). God can do anything, can't he? By his glorious power he reaches down and makes us what we need to be. In the face of difficult circumstances he gives us an injection of spiritual determination. He teaches us that cloudy times bring much-needed rain—rain that keeps us from wilting. When we stumble in our weakness, he makes us strong. Then he teaches us how to fly above the clouds.

As the famous reformer Martin Luther once said: "Faith is a great art and doctrine, which no saint has learned and fathomed fully unless he has found himself in despair, in the anguish of death, or in extreme peril." Graduate, that is where you will see God. Without the will to win, you will never get off the ground.

In fact, if you have the will to win, you're a winner already. I think even Vince Lombardi would agree that's true.

1️⃣6️⃣ **Signs**

Star Trek

The sun will be turned to darkness and the moon to blood before the coming of the great and dreadful day of the LORD. [Joel 2:31]

One day early in 1991 I was getting a haircut at the local beauty salon. I always get my haircuts there. Carol cuts my hair with a razor after a relaxing shampoo. It's one of life's little highlights. Anyway, while I was getting my haircut, a few of the other patrons were talking about Operation Desert Storm and the end of the world. I perked up my ears.

90

"This is the beginning of Armageddon," said lady number one.

"Yes, and Saddam Hussein is the Antichrist," said the second.

"And think about all those recent earthquakes and famines," said the third.

"I must admit it's all rather scary," said Carol, joining the conversation.

I contemplated jumping in at that point, but contained myself. Getting a haircut is so pleasant that I didn't want to spoil my comfort. Besides, the comments were getting interesting.

"Well, it bothers me that so much uproar is going on over there in the Middle East," said the hairdresser of lady number one. "Israel is right in the middle of all the action. That sure fits what is supposed to happen at the end of the world."

That term, "end of the world," amuses me. Do people actually believe that one day the world is going to go Boom! and blow up? Their recent ancestors probably believed the earth is flat. True, Jesus talked about the "last days," but the end of the world is not going to happen in a Custer's Last-Stand kind of battle. Scripture talks about seven years of "great tribulation" and "the millennium"—the reign of Jesus Christ on earth. I believe that's at least 1,007 more years before the *real* end of the world.

Back to the beauty salon. "I'm sure we'll keep seeing more and more soldiers from all countries gather there for one great big war," the first lady spoke up.

"Yes, and that Antichrist, Hussein, will finally get his judgment," the second lady said confidently.

That was enough for me to butt in: "You know, when Adolf Hitler started World War Two, almost everybody was sure *he* was the Antichrist." I spoke in a quiet tone, and a hush fell over the room. A man was interrupting the beauty-salon chat! (Equal rights works both ways, I think.)

I continued, "American Christians were so sure Hitler was the Antichrist that they came up with peculiar mathematical formulas that they applied to the letters of the alphabet. Hitler supposedly spelled out "666" mathematically. The longer the war dragged on, the more convinced folks were that the end of the world was coming. And, remember, the Jews were in the middle of things then, too. Hitler's henchmen were senselessly killing them by the thousands."

Carol was pleased by my invasion into the prophecies of the curler crowd. With frowns, they tried not to look aghast at my comments. But I could see Carol's dimples growing at each side of her grin. She exchanged knowing glances with the hairdresser of lady number two, who was determined to keep the debate alive: "Well, as terrible as that war was, it wasn't fought in the Persian Gulf."

"Maybe this does signal the return of Jesus Christ," I answered. Ah-ha! *Jesus.* He is the real issue. Right? Suddenly it seemed apparent that every person in the beauty salon was a believer. "I think it's good that we look for his coming," I added.

"I just don't think we should trust that Saddam Hussein," the second lady replied.

"Neither do I," I agreed. "But we must be careful not to fall into the same trap as other Christians have. Many have declared the end of the world, and the world did not end. Others have named the Antichrist, but named the wrong person or made other bold predictions and were later embarrassed." My eyes were closed as I finished talking. I was really enjoying this haircut.

"Well, one thing is sure," said the lady who had mentioned the earthquakes and famines, "with all that's happening in the world, the Lord must be coming soon."

That was a point we all agreed with.

What do you believe about the second coming of Jesus Christ? Do you expect him here soon? Do you expect him at all? If you spend long enough time with the prophets, you will be convinced Jesus is coming back to earth. You will also discover that his return to this planet is foreshadowed by a number of events: wars, rumors of wars, earthquakes, false Christs, ecological damage, rampant immorality, increased crime. And Jews will be hated and return to their homeland. Above all, there will be a blatant falling away from the truths found in God's Word.

The prospect of Jesus' return in our lifetime should help us concentrate on a couple of required courses:

Keep a clean house. If company were coming to visit, would you leave a filthy mess lying about? Probably not. You'd drag out the vacuum sweeper and straighten the clutter. Sure, even lazy housekeepers make a little effort at spritzing up their homes when company is coming. Well, Jesus is coming. Who would want him to find their life all a mess? Believe me, there won't be any last-minute time to run around brushing the dirt under the rug when he arrives. Every hidden thing will be revealed in that day. Humbling thought for all of us, huh?

Prepare others. The evangelism explosion of the '70s is pretty much a thing of the past. That's too bad. Today's believers act as if witnessing is something we must do undercover. Like we're members of a secret society. But if Jesus is coming soon—and signs indicate that he is—we don't have time to be secretive about the Good News. A storm is brewing, and we know the way to the shelter. Use a blowhorn to spread the message loud and clear! Don't expect the unsaved masses to read your mind.

Start in the beauty salon. Folks there love prophets. Call Saddam Hussein the Antichrist and see if that doesn't fire things up and curl the patrons' hair without using a styling gel.

Prophecies of Catastrophe

Jonah and Hosea

It may serve as a comfort to us in all our calamities and affliction that he that loses anything and gets wisdom by it is a gainer by the loss.
    Sir Roger L'Estrange

Men stumble over the truth from time to time, but most pick themselves up and hurry off as if nothing happened.
    Winston Churchill

17 Failure

Moby Dick

But Jonah ran away from the LORD and headed for Tarshish. He went down to Joppa, where he found a ship bound for that port. After paying the fare, he went aboard and sailed for Tarshish to flee from the LORD. [Jon. 1:3]

Richard Lemon tells about a truly bizarre occurrence in an article entitled "The Uncertain Science." A mental institution in a Paris suburb during World War II housed 154 patients who were considered by the best psychiatrists to be hopelessly insane. One night the bombs were going off all over the city, when suddenly the walls of the hospital were shelled and demolished. In the mass confusion, all the "crazies" managed to escape. Scary thought, huh?

Many years later, when all of the patients were finally tracked down, psychiatrists were amazed to find that 86 of the 154 had completely recovered and were living full, happy lives. Over fifty percent of those supposedly incurable failures weren't failures at all!

In the heading of our chapter we have the most important part of Jonah's biography: He took the wrong road. This prophet was mapping a blueprint for failure. Not that he was aware of what he was doing—not from the standpoint of ruining his life, that is. I'm sure Jonah knew that "playing tag" with God is never a profitable business, but I'm not so certain he knew what his actions would cost him. I don't think he could predict what a miserable failure he was becoming.

This is true of all the thousands who plod along day after day, caught in the rut of ignoring God. The novelist Ellen Glasgow said, "The only difference between a rut and a grave are their dimensions." Jonah spent his years as a prophet in a rut. While his preaching was sometimes powerful and effective, Jonah was a failure as a man because his heart wasn't in his work; he questioned his mission in life and was a reluctant participant. Scripture never says whether Jonah ever snapped out of his I-feel-sorry-for-myself attitude, but I doubt he did. Jonah's prejudices and preferences were more important to him than God's will. Ultimately he paid a dear price for that and learned that minimal effort sets one up for maximum failure. "Success" is one of the minors in the College of Life, but if you step into the classroom of the whale, I believe you can earn a straight A. If Jonah could speak, he might share these three thoughts with you:

Success is a deceiving term. Doing your best is more important than being the best. Some people think that being on top is a true measure of success. That's not always the case. Suicide rates are highest among professional people who "have it all." The price for such success is often stress, depression, and serious problems with relationships. Is that what you call success? Me neither. Please do not misunderstand my words. I encourage you to pursue your dreams and reach for lofty goals. I'm not suggesting that you'll be a failure if you come short of your high hopes. My point is that real success begins with a genuine love for God; real failure begins on the road to Tarshish, heading away from God. Don't be deceived by what the world calls success. Likewise, don't give up values *they* think are foolishness. Unbelievers consider faith in God a foolish creed. If you join them, all your worldly achievements can't prevent your ultimate failure.

Fear of failure is worse than failure itself. Quentin Crisp said, "It's no good running a pig farm for thirty years while saying, 'Really I was meant to be a ballet dancer.' By that time, pigs will be your style." Here's some simple math: Risk plus failure can equal success. You probably can think of dozens of things that keep people from taking a risk, but all of them boil down to fear. Early in life we all learn that failure brings criticism. Because criticism hurts, like Pavlov's dog we avoid failure-prone activities in fear of that potential pain. Fear, then, is a killer of success. But bowing to fear of failure is self-defeating, because failure is a necessary ingredient in any recipe for success. People who never learn how to handle being down don't know how to act when they are up. Success corrupts them. They come to expect it as their due, rather than appreciate it as a blessing from God. Even a series of failures is often a step-by-step plan to success. Sometimes failure *plus* failure *plus* failure equals success. To avoid the possibility of failure is to miss an opportunity at success. Too many people operate pig-style—slop in the morning and slop in the evening. Like Jonah, their lives are dominated by fear and trembling.

Failure is just a beginning. Did Henry Ford's crew build a V-8 engine on the first try? Was the first flight of the Wright brothers a dazzling feat? Do many actors win an Academy Award for their first performance? Does an artist usually become famous after painting his or her first "masterpiece"? Did Alex Bell's first try at telecommunications work? Was the first computer as fast at data processing as the new 386's? Was Walt Disney a rich man before founding the reknowned Disneyland? Can a golfer expect to win the Masters on the first try? Say "No" to all those questions. The point is obvious: You've gotta start somewhere. Success almost always starts with at least one failure. I received a couple of handfuls of rejection letters before my first magazine article was accepted and published. If fear of failure had overcome me, I'd probably be doing something else besides writing. Go ahead, give yourself a chance to fail. At least it's a start.

Jonah, on the other hand, failed on purpose. He headed in the opposite direction from where God wanted him to go. That's grounds for being admitted to a crazy mega-farm for failures, where millions have been reluctant residents. Thank goodness some, unlike Jonah, have escaped, recovered, and gone on to succeed.

18 Emptiness

Broken Arrow

Now, O LORD, take away my life, for it is better for me to die than to live. [Jon. 4:3]

I love classical music. Yes, that's a bold thing to admit to the Hip-Hop and Rap Generation, but it's true. My favorite composer? Sergei Rachmaninoff—probably because of the drama that oozes from his romantic interludes.

Ludwig van Beethoven ranks right up there, too. I'm not sure what amazes me more about him, his music or his legend. Plagued by depression and unhappiness, Mr. B. began losing his hearing as a young man. By the age of forty-eight, he was totally deaf, but five years later he completed his masterful Ninth Symphony. This marvel of music never heard a note of that composition; he just let it sing across the vocal cords of his genius. Pardon me, but such talent seems quite beyond the reach of the Madonnas of today's music.

Still another classical performer helps me lie still at the end of a grueling day. He was a tender five years old when he wrote an advanced concerto for the harpsichord. Before he was a teenager, he had composed several violin sonatas and a full opera. He lived only thirty-five years, but he finished over six hundred musical works! His name? Joannes Chrysostomus Wolfgangus Theophilus (Amadeus) Mozart. No wonder everybody just calls him Mozart or Amadeus.

Mozart's story, however, ended on a sour note. Despite his fame, the young composer had many enemies and died in relative obscurity. He was a poor money manager and was buried in an unmarked grave in a paupers' cemetery. No one knows exactly where. No headstone for the man now considered by many to be the greatest composer of all time. On the day of his funeral, a pelting rainstorm prevented his friends from attending the gravesite. What an empty way to leave this world. Very sad, I think.

Emptiness can happen on all levels of life. We hear talk of the homeless and that people are suffering in our world with no food to eat. We read stories of people abused by their governments and deprived of the barest necessities. But all this seems far from us. Face it, graduate, most of us Americans are spoiled rotten. Many of you are worried about whether you'll be able to afford a car next year. Do you have any concept of what it means to have nothing?

Spiritual poverty is another story, though. As a nation we're developing some firsthand expertise in that area. America is truly rich in technology, but growing poorer in godly wisdom and strength of character. If it's happening to us nationally, then it must be happening to us individually. That may be why you received this book. Someone is concerned about your spiritual well-being and doesn't want you to end up in rags when it comes to the things of God.

Too bad somebody didn't look out for Jonah like that. He was such a rebellious prophet that God needed to teach him a lesson. Incidentally, have you ever explored exactly how things went awry for Jonah? He didn't want to preach to Nineveh. It wasn't that he didn't want to serve God. Jonah hated the Ninevites because they were heathens and therefore enemies of Israel. He thought God should show no compassion for pagans. He was prejudiced, plain and simple. When God didn't give the rebel his way, off he went in the opposite direction from Nineveh. Near the end of the story we read the words that head our chapter. Not a flamboyant closing, huh? Professor Jonah teaches us what *not* to do—by his own example. Consider these truths about emptiness:

Emptiness does not come overnight. Jonah must have been an accomplished and persuasive orator or God wouldn't have selected him to go to Nineveh. Bear in mind, this was a highly intelligent nation of people. At least they thought they were. Jonah was God's choice, so he must have had something going for him. When Jonah finally did arrive in town, he was a tremendously effective evangelist. The result of his campaign was a major national revival. Still, Jonah was unhappy. Day by day he grew more bitter. The rebel did not like his cause. He was not committed to what he was sent to do. Even though God had given Jonah a second chance by saving him from the whale's belly, the ingrate still didn't get the point. Although Nineveh did turn from its evil ways, Jonah kicked up a fuss about God's sparing the city his wrath. Gradually Jonah lost his will to live. When his brief story ends, Jonah is destitute and out of touch with God and everyone else. Believe me, this can happen to anybody. Do not set yourself adrift. The farther out to sea you float, the harder it is to paddle back in. It is foolish to assume that a rescue boat will come along to save you. Beware of shifting tides and deceptively calm breezes.

Emptiness is a shocking experience. The prodigal son stared into the pig trough one day and wondered how he ever came to such a horrible existence. Want to hear a gross confession? I've been tempted a time or two to taste Winston's Milkbone dog biscuits. (Winston is our three-pound Yorkie.) Honestly, I have yet to eat one and doubt I will ever bring myself to chew up doggie treats, but I have wondered what they taste like. If the truth be known, I bet many of you have had your curiosity about pet food, too. I mean, are we missing out on something? But eat with pigs? No, thank you. That is not a temptation for me. If anything, it's disgusting and shocking. Yet the prodigal had to crawl in the mud with them before he came to his senses. Sounds like something you would see on "60 Minutes." Jonah, too, learned that the price of willful disobedience is painful. You probably won't land at the bottom of the sea but may be surprised at how far down you are capable of going. So why get on the slide to begin with?

Emptiness comes just before brokenness. At least for some people it does. Thank God for brokenness. Psalm 34:18 promises that God is "close to the brokenhearted." And Professor Isaiah foretold of Jesus's coming to bind up the brokenhearted (Isa. 61:1). Sometimes the only way up is down. I mean, some people aren't about to change until they have hit bottom. Unfortunately, it takes time and know-how to put Humpty Dumpty back together again, so think twice before taking H.M.S. *Jonah.*

Empty vessels can be filled again. There are two ways to become "empty." Slowly pour yourself out in service for others, or just throw the cup on the ground. Of course, if you break the cup, be prepared for a glue job. And you might have a few leaks. Even then, God will use you again if you are willing to revisit the repair shop. Far better it is to be filled and emptied in normal service. Refills come much easier that way.

Brilliant as he was, Mozart shattered himself on the ground through unwise alliances and wasteful spending. That is a tragedy. Once he was so full of promise, but he finished a broken man. And no one was there to say "Good-bye."

19 Calamity

Fatal Attraction

They sow the wind and reap the whirlwind. . . .
[Hos. 8:7]

W̶hen it comes to embarrassment, nothing surpasses stumbling. We've all had one of those unexpected moments of injured pride. There you were walking along and minding your own business—feeling pretty cool about life and how you looked and how sharp you were dressed—when Bam! You tripped and fell flat on your face. Sometimes it's ice that gets you. Sometimes it's a little rise in the pavement or loose footing on the stairs. The worst, however, is when it's nothing. Sometimes we just stumble for no reason. Ever done that? I have, and I usually glare at my shoes or the ground as if it was their fault.

Ever seen another person stumble? Shame on me, but that is sometimes funny stuff. Of course, I don't find it amusing if a person is hurt in a fall. It's the pride-crushers I laugh at. When toddlers flip over, it can be cute; when adults go down, it can be hilarious. I especially chuckle when famous people stumble. Isn't that a terrible admission of human nature? The camera lens is pointed directly at them when Oops! The goof-ups of important people uncover their humanity. We suddenly realize they are no different from us common folks. Our average lives somehow seem more meaningful.

Unfortunately, most of us stumble spiritually at least once in our lifetime. We just blow it. Often such a fall comes on the heels of great victories and achievements. Mountaintop experiences can make us think too highly of ourselves. Pride and belly flops make good dance partners. Many spiritual klutzes have the courage to stand up and continue the walk of faith, but some of them just stay down, indulging in self-pity and useless moans of regret.

One night a killer tornado hit a small Kansas town about three hours south of where I live. Scary thing is, two weeks before, I was on assignment in a city less than twenty minutes away from where the devastation struck. Some residents lost everything. One woman was digging through the rubble after the tornado was gone and found her husband dead beneath what used to be the home they shared. For miles around you could see total ruination. What once was a neighborhood looked like matches spilled out of their boxes. Absolute calamity.

Old-timers call tornadoes "the whirlwind." I'm not one to thump the Bible and holler at people about hellfire and damnation. Maybe there's a place for that, but I don't feel called to be a messenger of judgment. (You should note that almost every prophet had a very negative side to his message.) Anyway, back to the whirlwind. I'm not even going to try to explain why "natural disasters" and other evils happen, but God *does* see to it that people reap what they sow. Hosea said it in his prophecy, and Paul repeated it in one of his letters to the early church (Gal. 6:7). You can't mock God.

I'm not suggesting that the people of Andover, Kansas, deserved to have a tornado rip their town to shreds. Gracious no! What happened there only serves to illustrate how awful a disaster can be. Here's the bottom line: Those who plant evil—"sow the wind"—harvest disappointment, failure, and sometimes catastrophe. It is one thing to stumble. It is quite another to take a tragic plunge into wickedness.

Calamity plays no favorites; it gladly falls on anyone foolish enough to dare the wind. And it keeps records on unbelievers and believers alike. Calamity is like the agriculture business. It's all in the seeds. (I'm speaking spiritually, of course.) Some say that youth is a time to sow wild oats. They say, "Be experimental. Live it up. Be a party-hearty." Let me ask you: If you sow wild seeds, what do you expect to reap? Two or three or four years from now, what will come your way? If you listen to those who enjoy "blowing in the wind," will it surprise you if a tornado sweeps through your life?

Hosea warned people about spiritual shipwrecks. About disaster. He tried to tell them that a sudden striking hurricane rarely misses those who are so busy playing that they can't run to safety in time. The more gleefully they walked on the wild side, the greater the chance they would stumble into the midst of a raging, inescapable storm. Doesn't it stand to reason that those who live recklessly have wrecks?

108

Oh, incidentally, calamity doesn't always strike with brash sirens and sudden winds as loud as freight trains. Sometimes calamity slowly spreads out as it grows, kind of like that kudzu vine in the South that strangles everything in its path. At first you don't even notice it. Then it covers a fence. Then the chimney and walls. Gradually it snakes its way along the gutter and over the roof. It begins to choke sunlight from the windows. On the ground the vine kills anything that grows near it, smothering the life from any healthy plant that threatens to share its space. Eventually it takes over everything. Calamity is sometimes like that—a creeping menace.

Maybe you think calamity only happens to people who shun God and deny his existence. But spiritual disasters can happen to believers, too—believers who stumble and don't get up except to stumble again on the wrong road. Or believers who come to enjoy being down so much that they don't bother to get up. Then others will weep for them:

Once a true believer
Once there was a fire in your soul
You were the epitome of blessed faith astir
With thirst for holiness
And hunger for the Word
Now you move in other circles
To the beat of different drums
And I see only glimpses of the one you used to be
The inspiration that you were to me.
I miss the way His love would dance within your eyes
I miss the way His heart was the soul of your life
And somewhere in the saddest part of heaven's room
Our Father sheds a tear for you
He's missing you, too.

Michael W. Smith

If you've stumbled, stand up and brush yourself off. Don't worry about who's looking or what they think. God loves you. He will help you find your balance. And he will be your shelter from the whirlwind.

Prophecies of Honor

Amos and Micah

*We laugh at honor and are shocked
to find traitors in our midst.*
                    C. S. Lewis

*I would much rather have men ask
why I have no statue, than why I
have one.*
                    Marcus Porcius Cato

...AND FURTHERMORE, I PREDICT THE SUN WILL SHINE SOME TIME THIS MONTH.

20 Prediction

Great Expectations

But you, Bethlehem Ephrathah, though you are small among the clans of Judah, out of you will come for me one who will be ruler over Israel, whose origins are from of old, from ancient times. [Mic. 5:2]

What makes a prophet a prophet? A biblical prophet was one who spoke under divine inspiration, *fore*-telling and *forth*-telling the Word of God. Prophets predicted coming events and proclaimed eternal truths. There are no prophets today, in that sense of the word.

One requirement for being a legitimate prophet of God is 100% accuracy of prediction (check out Deuteronomy 18:21–22). False prophets abuse truth by relying on faulty data, so they make lots of mistakes. In Old Testament times, soothsayers would watch the stars and offer predictions based on superstition and "witch magic." Some of them were pretty good at guesswork and received jobs working for kings.

You might remember that Daniel was called on to interpret a dream for King Nebuchadnezzar. He wasn't summoned until after all the king's soothsayers had their shot at explaining the dream and forecasting its outcome. Finally Daniel was brought in, and he came up with the exact meaning. His predictions were totally accurate. Daniel was on his way to being a Gold Star prophet.

Popular tabloids, like what you see in the grocery-store check-out line, occasionally feature modern-day soothsayers. Jeanne Dixon is a well-known psychic whose predictions frequently appear in print. She is credited with having predicted the assassination of President Kennedy, among other historical events. She is not a prophetess, however, because she's "correct" about only 20% of the time (maybe less than that). Most of these psychic-types are running a scam. I don't pay them much attention.

Probably the most widely read modern soothsayer material is the daily horoscope. My guess is that every person who reads this chapter knows his or her sign of the zodiac. I'm an Aquarius—waterboy, which may explain why I like hot tubs so much. Anyway, horoscopes are hoaky business as far as I'm concerned. Have you ever checked out the accuracy of the predictions those dumb things make? Listen to this one. It's my horoscope for Saturday, April 11, 1991: "Today may be filled with distractions and inaccuracies. You could be gadding about to no avail. If you can stay put and relax, you've got it made."

Now isn't that special! How brilliant. Whose Saturdays are *not* filled with distractions? Who wouldn't have it made if they could "stay put and relax"? What would I have done without the dubious good fortune of having seen this horoscope? Would my life have been in complete disarray that Saturday?

Here's more earth-shattering advice from the same article:

> Don't rush blindly into residential matters. If you are planning to move, investigate before you invest. Scrutinize plumbing, wiring or improvements, leases or contracts. Also, builders, decorators and suppliers will tend to gloss over details, so be sure to inspect for any concealed flaws and schedule extra time for possible delays until after the 26th.

Sounds like a paragraph out of a home-buyers' guide instead of a horoscope. And look at that stuff. Investigate before investing—now there's a revolutionary idea. Before I read that horoscope, I just threw money hand over fist into investments that I knew nothing about. Then I started being careful. Just as I hope you caught my sarcastic tone, I hope you don't pay any mind to horoscopes. They are worthless.

In our lead verse for this chapter, we read one of the more famous prophecies of the Old Testament. It's what theologians refer to as a "messianic prophecy." That is, it relates directly to the life or ministry of Jesus Christ, the Messiah. There are hundreds of such predictions in the various books of the Old Testament. The one from Micah 5:2 is a perfect example of how specific the prophets were when they *fore*told a coming event.

Bear in mind what the people of Micah's day must have thought when he relayed God's message that Bethlehem would be the place where Israel's "ruler" would be born. They would have laughed. "Why there? Why in that little town? Ha! Ha! Ha!" Years later. . . . But we all know the story.

When Isaiah talked about the future ministry and crucifixion of Jesus, be sure that many people thought he was way off base. Today, of course, Christians are humbled by the truths contained in that passage of Scripture (Isa. 53).

What am I getting at? The distant voices of the prophets have something to say to us today. Two points and I'm out of here for now. These are simple but important thoughts you should chew on for a while. Don't just glance over them. Let these bits of wisdom sink into your hopeful heart.

All prophecies pertaining to the earthly life of Jesus have been fulfilled. That's right. Every last one. And there are several dozen referring to all sorts of things—from his mother, to his birthplace, to his ministry, to his death and resurrection. Not surprised? Well, this point isn't meant to surprise you, but rather to lead to a question: If all the prophecies about Jesus' first coming were perfectly fulfilled, isn't that good reason to believe all the prophecies about his *second* coming will be likewise fulfilled? The prophets promised the return of Christ to this earth. Dare we doubt them? Dare we dispute their predictions when they have yet to be wrong?

Fulfilled prophecy is like Vitamin B to our faith. It revives us in times of doubt and discouragement. Ever wonder if God is really there? Is he really listening? Does he even care? Remember this: He sent the prophets, and they made promise after promise that God kept. The apostle Peter tells us, "All the prophets testify about him [Jesus] . . ." (Acts 10:43). Let that feed your faith. Peter wrote in his later years that we have had the words of the prophets clarified by the life of Christ (2 Peter 1:19). The prophets' fulfilled predictions are steel reinforcements in the concrete of our faith. Their prophecies are unbreakable links in the long chain of truth.

I don't bother with horoscopes, but not just because they are related to the occult and speak nonsense most of the time. Rather, I have something better to show me the way. Something that holds a lot more meaning than "if you can stay put and relax, you've got it made."

21 Fairness

Tender Mercies

Hear this, you who trample the needy and do away with the poor of the land. . . . The LORD has sworn by the Pride of Jacob: "I will never forget anything they have done." [Amos 8:4, 7]

Few things challenge my sense of fairness as much as being a parent. As the father of two pre-adolescent children, I am constantly bombarded with situations where I'm expected to be prosecutor, judge, jury, and executioner. The legal cases may come at any moment. Last Friday, afternoon court was in session. I was relaxing with a good book on the family room couch when the contending parties came rushing downstairs seeking the wisdom of Solomon.

"Dad, Jared won't get out of my room," proclaimed my nine-year-old daughter, Sara, demanding immediate police action.

"She asked me to come into her room to begin with," answered the defendant, Jared, eighteen months her senior. Then came a countercharge: "And she kicked me."

At first I pretended not to pay attention. This is a usual practice for me, though I don't know why I act like I haven't heard the kids. Maybe I'm hoping they will go away. Marking my page, I turned my eyes upon the culprits who had disturbed my peace.

"What started this?" The official trial was underway with my first question.

"I told Jared to get out of my room and he wouldn't," Sara declared as she fought back tears. She probably wondered if she would get a fair hearing in this male-dominated courtroom, but my past record gave her reason to believe she would.

I glanced at Jared for his side of the story.

"We were playing in Sara's room, which was her idea, and she got mad and told me to get out," he explained.

"Said it just like that," I teased—"just said, 'Get out!'" They appreciated the humor. It took the edge off an earlier tense moment in this legalistic drama.

"Yeah," Jared giggled, and we all laughed.

"Why'd she want you out?" I asked.

"Well, we were playing—"

"Playing what?"

Jared hesitated. "We were jumping on the bed and wrestling." He obviously hated to admit that one.

"Jumping on the bed?" I questioned Sara, who had had run-ins with the law before on this charge.

"Yes," she whispered, her eyes turned downward.

"Why were you wrestling with your sister?" Here I returned to Jared, thinking it best to let Sara consider her situation for a moment.

"It's fun," he replied with a barely hidden grin. Out of the corner of my eye I could see that Sara had a grin to match.

"Don't tell me . . ." I cut to the chase, ". . . you were wrestling and having fun—jumping on the bed [I glanced at Sara] and somebody got hurt. And that somebody was Sara."

Sara nodded. The prosecution rested.

Jared sprang to his own defense. "Oh, yeah, then why did you kick me when I wouldn't leave? And then, why did you push me down and jump on me? Huh? Tell me that."

"Now let's calm down," I used a gentle tone.

"I didn't jump on you," Sara blurted back. "I stepped on you. Besides, you should have left my room."

"Whoa!" I halted the discussion in an unprecedented move. "You know that hitting, kicking, and other violence bring automatic punishment in our family, don't you?"

Sara must have hoped I had forgotten that rule. "Yes," she conceded.

I looked at Jared. Feeling compelled to go on, he said, "I should have left when she asked, and we shouldn't have been wrestling or jumping on the bed." With that, the defense rested.

The verdict was coming: "You both know we've covered this before. If you can't fairly settle your own problems, and I have to settle them for you, neither of you likes the outcome. Bedtime tonight is eight o'clock. If you finish your baths and straighten your rooms, you can read in bed for thirty minutes. Then it's lights out."

"But, Dad," they chimed in together, "it's Friday night. We never go to bed so early on Friday night." (Note the feeble attempt to plea-bargain.)

120

"Yes, I know. But this will give you an extra hour and a half to remember the intended purpose of mattresses."

Jared was dismissed. Sara stayed behind to discuss punishment for the kicking. Later we all talked about forgiveness and took a few moments to restore our love connection. Then I read to them for a while. Justice was served. By that time I was tired and ready for bed myself.

Fairness is a pain in the neck. Really, it is. Don't misunderstand me. Fairness is one of life's "majors," but it's a tough course. Everybody expects fair treatment, but it's not always forthcoming. I want to be treated fairly, don't you? Give me my part of the driving lane. Don't cut in the grocery line in front of me. Be reasonable with the gasoline prices. Make the rich pay more taxes than I do. Keep the criminals out of my neighborhood. (Is that spoiled-American talk or what?)

Life isn't like that. Drivers are rude; shoppers take too many items into the express lane; oil barons raise gas prices arbitrarily; politicians create tax loopholes for the rich; and lenient judges give criminals probation instead of jail time. Fairness is a hard thing to manage or even define. Especially in a world made up of a bunch of "special interest" groups with conflicting demands.

Amos, the fig-picker, had problems in his day, too. The poor people were being trampled underfoot by the rest of society. Sounds like a page out of today's news, when you consider all the homeless who are wandering our streets. Yet congregations build million-dollar cathedrals, but have no shelters for the homeless. Some churches spend thousands on organs, pianos, choir robes, and sheet music, but have no program to feed the hungry and clothe the naked. I'm telling you, God doesn't like it. And he won't forget it.

If Amos were here, though, I think he would tell us not to expect fairness all the time. But he would also remind us to treat others as we want to be treated. He might even deliver a hot sermon or two about big-time churchianity to disrupt our moral complacency.

God is watching us, and it is unwise to test his patience. He sometimes sends his children to bed early, too. Fortunately for us, he tempers his justice with mercy. I pondered this as I turned out the lights at 8:30 last Friday.

22 Obedience

The King and I

With what shall I come before the LORD and bow down before the exalted God? Shall I come before him with burnt offerings, with calves a year old?
[Mic. 6:6]

The other day I heard a short anecdote told by a mother whose daughter had called her at work. Apparently the girl had just arrived home from school and wanted to check in with her mother. The ensuing conversation illustrates how many of us feel about receiving extra duties.

"Hi, Mom! What do you want me to do today?"

"I thought we decided that last night," Mom replied. "You were going to wash the dishes, mop the kitchen floor, and clean the bathroom."

After a few moments of silence, the response came back, "Oops, wrong mom." Click.

Sounds like a conversation that could have as easily taken place between Jesus and one of today's uncommitted disciples. He might say, "I bid you to follow me with all your heart and serve me with love and perseverance." And the disciple on the other end of the line, in a hurry to be off to the music concert, would reply, "Oops, wrong Savior."

Micah had to deal with the problem of disobedience in his day. Every prophet did. In the B.C. (before Christ) days, people were preoccupied with farming, family life, building communities, and minding their personal pleasures. They paused only long enough to offer God a shekel or two. Then it was back to "distorting all that is right" and "judging for a bribe" (see Mic. 3:9–10). Honor was gone— because obedience was gone.

Obedience is a major issue for every graduate to consider. Over the next few years your life will change dramatically. Most of you will move away from home, either to an out-of-town college or your own apartment. You will exercise independence and learn to order your own priorities. There will be no one urging you out of bed on Sunday mornings for church. When the pastor calls for servants to help distribute food and clothing to the poor, you will have to decide whether to participate. You will be faced with numerous opportunities to serve others out of obedience to Christ. The choice will be up to you. Maybe a group in your dormitory or fraternity house will need a Bible-study leader or a prayer captain. Only you will know if God is urging you to get involved with his work. Only you will know if you're being obedient.

If you thought high school was busy, you ain't seen nothin' yet. I speak from experience. My years from nineteen to twenty-four were a blur of activity: I earned my degree, changed jobs five times, married, started my first pastorate, bought my first home, doubled the size of my family by having two children, bought and traded three cars, and started a retirement account. In those days I counted each day as a precious commodity. Now I don't even bother counting the days; they pass faster than I can keep track. I concentrate on knowing which month it is and wonder how some people find time to get a tan that lasts the year around.

As God turns up the speed on your life-ometer, where will Christian service and personal obedience fit in? Will you adapt your *major* decisions to his will, or will you seek to feed your ego? Will you filter your personal goals through God's sieve, or will you forge ahead on your own? If God leads you to change your goals, will you? Here is where the rubber meets the road. When you consider these and other important questions about the direction of your life, remember the four aspects of obedience to God:

Obedience is better than gifts. Samuel, who had been called by God to serve as judge and prophet in Israel, confronted King Saul with this basic principle of obedience. He told the wayward leader, "To obey is better than sacrifice, and to heed is better than the fat of rams" (1 Sam. 15:22). God wants our good works, but not without our hearts. Our gifts are meaningless if we view them as ransom to buy us out of genuine discipleship. Too many Christians are wrapped up in playing religious games. They come to Sunday worship and financially support the work of the church, but experience only nominal change in their daily lives. Obedience to God is an every-minute affair; it can't be segregated from the rest of a believer's attitude and experience.

Obedience means unselfishness. Those who obey Jesus must have others on their minds. They cannot be like a kid who, when shown a long list of chores, whines resentfully, "But I planned to play ball today!" The world will always be calling us to be somewhere else besides where God wants us. The world's playthings may seem much more interesting, but putting selfish desires aside is the mark of a true servant. God sends a zillion blessings to your address, but you have to be there to receive them.

Obedience requires involvement. Obedience doesn't say, "Here am I, Lord, but this time send Judy." It says, "Send *me.*" God's service calls for eager volunteers who willingly go where needed and take part in the work. Obedience is not limited to your private relationship with Jesus Christ. It is not merely a matter of inward surrender. Obedience is a roll-up-the-sleeves word. It means "Get busy!"

Obedience is the way to happiness. On the other hand, disobedience is the path to misery. Following the principles of God sounds like a life of drudgery to the unbelieving masses. But are they happy? You know, God's call to obedience is really a call to happiness and peace of mind. Caring for others, sharing the gospel, practicing the Word in your daily life—this daily menu has few "stress calories." You won't get spiritually flabby if these are part of your lifestyle. And where there is obedience, there is honor and a sense of accomplishment.

Let's close a little differently than usual. This is a subject worthy of private meditation. Poems do the trick for me when I'm feeling reflective. Give this one a read. It's from one of my favorite poets—"Anonymous." Think on these things:

> I had walked life's path with an easy tread,
> Had followed where comfort and pleasure led;

And then by chance in a quiet place—
I met my Master face to face.

With station and rank and wealth for goal,
Much thought for body but none for soul,
I had entered to win this life's mad race—
When I met my Master face to face.

I had built my castles, reared them high,
Till their towers had pierced the blue of sky;
I had sworn to rule with an iron mace—
When I met my Master face to face.

I met Him and knew Him, and blushed to see
That His eyes full of sorrow were fixed on me;
And I faltered, and fell at His feet that day
While my castles vanished and melted away.

Melted and vanished; and in their place
I saw naught else but my Master's face;
And I cried aloud; "Oh, make me meet
To follow the marks of Thy wounded feet."

My thought is now for the souls of men;
I have lost my life to find it again
Ever since alone in that holy place
My Master and I stood face to face.

Prophecies
of Character

Nahum, Zephaniah,
and Habakkuk

*Character consists of what you do on
the third and fourth tries.*
James A. Michener

*Talent is nurtured in solitude; char-
acter is formed in the stormy billows
of the world.*
Johann Wolfgang von Goethe

23 Habits

Moonstruck

But they were still eager to act corruptly in all they did. [Zeph. 3:7]

Dwight D. Eisenhower was an extraordinary military leader. The late Merle Miller, a careful student of the man affectionately called "Ike," once wrote: "Eisenhower took the trouble to seem ordinary, to appear guileless. But he did outmaneuver and outcommand almost everybody, including Winston Churchill, Charles de Gaulle and even Franklin Roosevelt." Pretty impressive record, wouldn't you agree?

To what did Eisenhower attribute his achievements? To an event that happened on October 31, 1900—Halloween night—in Abilene, Kansas. While his brothers were allowed to go trick-or-treating, ten-year-old Ike had to stay home. "You're too young to go out," his father told him. Little Ike burst into tears, ran into the yard, and began punching his fists against the trunk of an apple tree.

He remembered the event later: "My dad suddenly had me by the collar and I was getting a tanning." Ike was sent to bed immediately. After the boy had shed a few tears, his mother, Ida, came into his room with some godly advice. She told him, "He that ruleth his spirit is better than he that taketh a city." Sixty-six years later, Ike wrote, "I have always looked back on that conversation as one of the most valuable moments of my life."

Ruling one's own spirit—self-control—is the key to overcoming bad habits. It is also the detonator for starting good ones. Zephaniah was given the challenge of ministering to a generation dead-set on corruption. They loved sin far too much to give it up. They were addicted to it. It wasn't just that their actions were evil—corruption itself was their habitual way of thinking and responding to life. Zephaniah described them by saying that "the unrighteous know no shame" (Zeph. 3:5). Brazen depravity is a hard habit to break.

Explore a couple of questions with me. (If you want to search this subject further, take it to your Bible-study group for discussion.)

Why are bad habits and addictions so easily developed? We live in a society so swamped with apparently "unsolvable" problems that it almost seems to encourage addictive-type behavior as an escape mechanism. A recent estimate of all the "addicts" in our culture numbers those affected by addiction at over 131 million. That includes food, alcohol, gambling, sexual, and chemical addictions.

Americans are spoiled by the conveniences we enjoy. We have devices to simplify everything, to provide instant gratification. Yesterday I saw a secretary preparing a milkshake at her desk with a battery-operated mixer the size of a screwdriver. What next?

When life gets us down, quick-fix logic takes over. We want an easy solution and we want it now. What do too many of us do? We seek thrilling escapes and entertainment. Anything to medicate the problems of life or to make boredom go away. The result? Our values are swept into confusion. We become overextended and overcommitted. Worry nags at us. More escapism. As this cycle develops we begin to feel powerless, and our lives seem out of control. We learn to exploit some *thing* or *person* to feel good about life again. Slowly enough for us not to notice, habits turn into addictions. That's why ruling your spirit is much harder than taking a city.

Don't think addictions are confined to adults. A recent story reported that a mother discovered her dead teenage son, who was nude and hanging by his belt in the bathroom. His was one of nearly a thousand deaths last year from "autoerotic asphyxia." The boy was trying to increase the pleasure of masturbation by momentarily cutting off the flow of oxygen to his brain. He accidentally strangled himself. Habits know no boundaries; addictions show no favoritism.

How are habits and addictions best broken? Few people break a habit without the assistance of good supporters. Impulsive behaviors have a voice of their own, and they speak to us inwardly to say: "You need me. I bring you pleasure. Come now, I'm not so bad—and neither are you for keeping me around. You've tried to do without me before and couldn't. If you're worried that I'm not good for you, just cut back a little." Those who have a destructive habit or addiction to break need a cheerleader. One of the first steps is finding someone you can trust who will be honest and confidential, encouraging but nonjudgmental.

Habits can't be broken apart from sobriety. I'm not talking about booze (though that is a problem for thousands of young people). You must want to quit and one day decide to do so completely. Until that day the habit lives on. After that day the urge may still be there. But as you work toward being totally sober, it will slowly shrink in intensity. Whole books have been written on how to beat addictions, including the importance of replacing bad habits with good ones. The point of this chapter, though, is to start you thinking. And searching. And talking with others who may need help or who can offer assistance to you.

In July 1945, with victory in Europe achieved, General Eisenhower was greeted by a standing ovation as he entered London's ancient Guildhall to give an address. Here is an excerpt of what he said:

> Humility must always be the portion of any man who receives acclaim earned in the blood of his followers and the sacrifices of his friends. I am not a native of this land. I come from the very heart of America. In the superficial aspects, the town where I was reared is far separated from this great city. But neither London nor Abilene, sisters under the skin, will sell her birthright for physical safety, her liberty for mere existence.

Ike knew the difference between freedom and bondage. His first lesson came from the one-sentence sermon his mother whispered to him on the power of self-control—on that Halloween night when he began majoring in ruling his own spirit.

24 Consequences

Crimes and Misdemeanors

> *The LORD is slow to anger and great in power; the LORD will not leave the guilty unpunished. His way is in the whirlwind and the storm, and clouds are the dust of his feet.* [Nah. 1:3]

Listen to this incredible story. Three Northwest Airlines pilots were recently convicted of flying while under the influence of alcohol. One of the pilots actually offered his alcoholism as a defense! He claimed he wasn't impaired by the liquor because his longtime use of alcohol had helped him develop a high level of tolerance for the stuff. According to testimony at his trial, he guzzled more than fifteen rum and Cokes the night before the flight. The case is being appealed.

Newsweek presented these startling statistics about pilots who drink and fly:

More than 10,000 of the 700,000 licensed U.S. pilots have drunken-driving records.

More than 1,200 airline pilots have been treated for alcoholism and returned to duty in the past 15 years.

Between 5 and 10 percent of general-aviation pilots killed in plane crashes each year have alcohol in their blood.

Six commuter and air-taxi accidents between 1980 and 1988 were attributed solely or in part to pilot drinking.

And my friends wonder why I hate to fly! The only thing I like about being in an airplane is getting off. Airplanes are cramped and uncomfortable. The bathrooms are tiny. The person next to you is usually weird. The windows are hard to see through. The food is boring. The bags of peanuts are too small. The takeoffs and landings are terrifying—much more ridiculous than skydiving (which I would never attempt), because at least skydivers have a parachute. And, tell me, how smart is it to put that much faith in someone you don't know, can't see, and can't talk to? I figure I'll die in a plane crash as the consequence of not listening to my inner voice of reason.

The inner voice of reason is important, you know. All airplane humor aside, God speaks to us in our conscience. That "still small voice" is our link with spiritual safety. If we shrug off the cautions we hear, we cannot escape the consequences of having played deaf. Consequences—good and bad—are inevitable, which means they are also a major subject in life's curriculum.

In his book *Growing Strong in the Seasons of Life,* Charles Swindoll describes a brand of human who defies all good sense by having no fear of the natural consequences that follow stupid choices:

> There's not a dad in America who'd let his daughter date a convicted murderer. . . . Or encourage his boy to wash windows at San Quentin.
>
> I mean, some things make no sense at all. Like lighting a match to see if your gas tank is empty. Or stroking a rhino to see if he's tame. Man, that's lethal! They've got a name for nuts who try such stunts. Victims. Or (if they live to tell the story) just plain *stupid.*
>
> And yet there's a strange species of Christian running loose today who flirts with risks far greater than any of the above. That's right. And they will do so with such a calm face you'd swear they had ice water in their veins. You could never guess by a glance they are balancing on the thin edge of disaster. Without a pole. And without a net.

Nahum the prophet had some startling news for these tightrope-walkers: "You're going to fall off the rope. The landing will not be pretty." Believe it or not, God holds all of us accountable for our choices. Nahum told his congregation just that. They didn't listen, so God rolled through their lives riding storm clouds of judgment. The plain truths of Nahum's message are simple and time-proven. Mark them down where they can often refresh your memory.

Every action has a consequence. If you do right, blessings come from it; if you do evil, pain comes. As long as that principle has been around, you'd think more earth-dwellers would take note of it. But they don't. Our courts are backlogged, and our jails are overflowing. Do the criminals slow down? Our country is in serious debt, but we keep borrowing to cover an inflated budget. When will we wise up and hear Nahum shouting for us to come out of the dark? And when will believers awaken to the toll that is due for wasting years in a love affair with the world?

God takes care of the consequences. He has a long memory. I'll leave it at that. But review chapters 21 and 22!

I should be concerned with my consequences, not anybody's else's. Be careful about sorting through what you think will happen to So-and-So for doing such-and-such. That is God's business. And don't use the influence and example of others as an excuse for sinning. Scripture nowhere gives the impression that God sets free anyone who is busy pointing a finger at the other guy. We behave like foolish children if we expect our Father to let us go because it was "Johnnie's" idea to do it. I am responsible for my choices. I am not responsible for other people's choices. If I want to lie down in green pastures, I cannot be my own shepherd.

"What goes up must come down"—that's the elementary fact of consequences. And that's exactly why I hate to fly.

25 Poise

The Taming of the Shrew

The Sovereign LORD is my strength; he makes my feet like the feet of a deer, he enables me to go on the heights. [Hab. 3:19]

A woman on maternity leave visited her office to show off her newborn infant. Everyone gathered around the weary and sleep-deprived woman to offer praises and cuddly-coos to the little one. Seven-year-old "big brother" also accompanied mother and babe.

"Mommy, can I have some money to buy some soda pop?" the boy asked politely.

"Is that all you can say?" she said, somewhat impatiently.

With unruffled charm and respect, the boy replied, "You're thin and beautiful and I love you a lot."

The woman reached in her purse with a smile and handed her son the money.

That boy had poise. And he wasn't short of charm either. One dictionary defines poise as a state of being "pleasantly tranquil, well composed, and graciously tactful under pressure." I'd say the lad must have been a dedicated poise-practitioner. Can you imagine how he will sweet-talk his mother when he's a teenager? It wouldn't surprise me if he were elected president someday.

One of the strangest love stories ever told shows us the value of poise as a diplomatic tool. William Shakespeare's comical romance about Petruchio and Katherine, *The Taming of the Shrew,* masterfully reveals the premium we should place on poise. And it gives us a good howl in the process. Petruchio was in love with Kate, a brawling brute of a woman. She was a shrew. That's not a title of glory, believe me. Centuries ago, "shrew" was a curse word (and probably still is). A shrew is also an animal in the rat family that looks a lot like a mole. In Kate's case, a shrew is a very ill-tempered woman.

Lesser souls would have opted for a quieter life's companion. Not Petruchio. He is drawn to Kate. He admires her spirit and acts with dignified poise to charm her. And a considerable amount of wit. The starting premise of the story is that Kate's younger sister is in love, but cannot be married until her older sister weds. This custom has Kate's father worried, because he fears his shrewish daughter will never be chosen by any man in his right mind. At first Kate spurns Petruchio's calculated attempts to win her heart. She does not believe him. In the end, of course, his unflappable poise conquers her unruliness. Kate's heart is melted to butter, and she and Petruchio live happily ever after. Rent the movie version for some fun and laughs. It's much better than what most moviemakers are coming out with today.

I think poise is also the underlying truth in the verse in Habakkuk— "He makes my feet like the feet of a deer." I think we can safely say that Mr. H. wasn't alluding to a potential victory at the Boston Marathon. If you search the context of the verse, you will find the prophet offering a prayer of praise and adoration to our great God. No wonder he fancied himself as graceful as a deer. He was *poised,* calmly prepared to receive God's blessing.

How does one acquire poise? Does it come through knowledge? From years of applying oneself in a classroom? Certainly not. I like the story of the professor who overheard students discussing the difficulty of their program at the Naval Postgraduate School in Monterey, California. "Don't worry too much about your grades," he counseled. "When you think you know everything, they give you a bachelor's degree. Then, when you realize that you don't know anything, they give you a master's. And when you find out that you don't know anything, but neither does anyone else, they give you a doctorate."

Fortunately, it doesn't have to take that long to fulfill the requirements for majoring in poise. What it does take, however, is careful attention to poise's key ingredients. Stir these traits into how you relate to others and enjoy the amazing results:

Composure. Being cool, calm, and collected—that's what poise is all about. Don't you think the prophets are ideal examples of these very qualities? These guys were not on many invitation lists to Israel's best parties. They brought a ton of bad news people didn't care to hear. In the face of rejection, scoffing, belittling comments, and outright hatred, these servants didn't waiver. Yes, a few, like

Jeremiah, wept, but only out of compassion and disappointment, not because of fear or weak character. Day after day, they held the standard high when others blatantly mocked and openly rebelled. Through faith and obedience they remained composed. And without Right Guard, I might add.

Tactfulness. If tactfulness is "saying the right thing at the right time," the prophets had earned their master's. But if tactfulness means ruffling no feathers, they weren't so successful. Poise keeps one from lashing back against offensive remarks. The prophets showed good savvy there. But they could be blunt, bold, and penetrating with their words. Yet even that requires a certain amount of poise. Although saying the hard thing is relatively easy, saying it well is more difficult. Tactfulness, then, is the courage to say the right thing at the right time even while others are casting aspersions. Poise tunes out the hecklers and speaks the truth without shame.

Silence. We generally picture the prophets preaching, don't we? That's not the case in the Habakkuk passage. He's alone, praying. A person with poise knows when to draw aside. It is not always the smart thing to speak out, no matter how persuasive you are. Wisdom is often sought from those of few words, those who choose carefully what they say. Scripture tells us that "even a fool is thought wise if he keeps silent" (Prov. 17:28). That reminds me of Mark Twain's witty quote: "It is better to remain silent and appear to be dumb, than to open your mouth and remove all doubt." The art of poise is mastered in silence. Motormouths have no poise. Braggarts have no poise. Pushy people have no poise. No, poise belongs to the one who controls his tongue (James 3). Out of silence grows composure; out of composure comes a golden word "aptly spoken" (Prov. 25:11).

142

Today's world is full of shrews, too. Even our churches have their share of them. Shakespeare would have a heyday. Unfortunately, there aren't enough Petruchios to go around. But if you'd like lessons in poise, find that little boy. He has the system down pat.

Prophecies of Perception

Haggai and Zechariah

Americans need to be warned about words and ideas which look much alike, but have different effects. For example, Americans often confuse size with importance, speed with progress, money with wealth, authority with wisdom, religion with theology, excitement with pleasure, and enthusiasm with hollering.

Carter Davidson

One man's justice is another's injustice; one man's beauty another's ugliness; one man's wisdom another's folly; as one beholds the same objects from a higher point of view.

Ralph Waldo Emerson

26 Curiosity

Cat on a Hot Tin Roof

I asked the angel who talked with me, "What are these, my lord?" He answered, "Do you not know what these are?" "No, my lord," I replied. [Zech. 4:4–5]

Christmas is my favorite holiday. As far back as I can remember, every Christmas I have had a good cry. A happy cry. May sound weird, but sometimes I like to cry. Does the soul good. Especially when it comes from feelings of warmth, joy, gratitude, security, and home. Christmas has all those feelings for me.

147

I still like to receive toys for Christmas. Last year my sister gave me a tiny pool table. I mean, *tiny.* It's about three inches by six inches. The cue stick looks like a long cigarette. The balls are nothing more than painted pellets. And the ball rack is smaller than a wedge of orange. She must have figured that since I never was any good at regulation-size pool, maybe I'd enjoy Munchkin-size pool. She was right.

Robert Fulghum is also a Christmas fanatic. In his popular book *All I Really Need to Know I Learned in Kindergarten,* he reveals a secret similar to my own:

> I do know what I want someone to give me for Christmas. I've known since I was forty years old. Wind-up mechanical toys that make noises and go round and round and do funny things. No batteries. Toys that need me to help them out from time to time. The old-fashioned painted tin ones I had as a child. That's what I want. Nobody believes me. It's what I want, I tell you.
>
> Well, okay, that's close, but not quite exactly it. It's delight and simplicity that I want. Foolishness and fantasy and noise. Angels and miracles and wonder and innocence and magic. That's closer to what I want.
>
> It's harder to talk about, but what I *really, really, really,* want is just this:
>
> I want to be five years old again for an hour.
>
> I want to laugh a lot and cry a lot.
>
> I want to be picked up and rocked to sleep in someone's arms, and carried up to bed just one more time . . . I want my childhood back.

When I was a little boy growing up at 618 Thornton Street, I thought being an adult was the most important thing in the world. Now I'm an adult and I think being a child is the most important thing in the world. Life is funny like that.

148

I guess the best part of being a kid is not knowing much. Adults don't really know much either, just enough to make them wish they were kids again, I think. But it's the "not knowing" part of life that makes living fun and interesting. That's probably another reason I like Christmas. I want to know what's inside all that wrapping paper. What is Santa bringing? (He still comes to see me.) What will he leave in my stocking? (Which has grown to the size of a small gunny sack.) Will he bring what I asked for? (Some of those little chocolate coins. And see if Godiva makes them now.) Christmas is a time for curiosity. It is a time of mystery.

Can you hear Zechariah's childlike curiosity in the verses at the top of the chapter? His tone is rich with an eagerness to learn. That's what curiosity is, and heaven help us when we lose that kind of enthusiasm. You know, something about adulthood seems to stifle the curiosity we once had as children. And no emotion is quite so dull as feeling you know what's coming next. When life turns monotonous and seems thoroughly predictable, something has to change. Knowing our need for learning something new all through life, God often sends trials to keep us guessing about the future. This is his way of putting the mystery back into our humdrum days.

I've come to appreciate curiosity. As a person who is recovering from the compulsion to have all the answers in neat little columns, I can tell you that life is sometimes more fun if you don't know the answers and do some exploring to find them. Especially if you let go of the pressure of *having* to know them.

Maybe this is just a "minor," nothing heavy. Yet I really think Zechariah touches on an important fact of life here. A few verses later we read God's question: "Who despises the day of small things?" (Zech. 4:10). Store the seemingly insignificant truths in the corner of your memory and mull them over later, when you can sit back and close your eyes and get the whole picture. Also consider these ideas:

You don't have to figure out everything. Doesn't it feel good to know that? You can be curious without finding out the answer. One of the wonders of being a child is knowing there's so much you don't know but plenty of time to learn. One of the pitfalls of being an adult is fearing you don't know enough and never will. Relax. Enjoy not knowing. Learning comes more naturally that way. By staying curious, you stay fresh. Life returns to being an unrehearsed adventure story.

You're more of a kid than you think. Even if you think you're more of a kid than you'd like to admit, you're even more of a kid than that. I'm a lot older than you are, and I realize I'm still a child in many ways. Our bodies grow up and our minds get fuller and more serious, but our hearts stay young. Deep down inside we never stop being boys and girls. Sometimes we forget that. Hurray for those who remember. God told us through Isaiah that "a little child will lead them" (Isa. 11:6). And Jesus said we must change and become like little children to enter his kingdom (Matt. 18:3). Don't get old at heart, whatever your age.

You must not lose your awe of life. You are a *created* being! What is more wonderful than that? God carved you out of nothing. One day, while the world was spinning around and planes were flying and the stock market was buzzing and people were dying, God breathed life into a tiny embryo—you. The world keeps on just as before, but now you are here. *Why* are you here? That question should be enough to keep you curious for the rest of your life.

Funny thing about that "Kindergarten" book by Robert Fulghum: My sister gave me that for Christmas, too. It came with the miniature pool table. Kind of a User's Guide, you might say.

27 Shortsightedness

Lost Horizon

*Now this is what the LORD Almighty says: "Give
careful thought to your ways. You have planted much,
but have harvested little. You eat, but never have
enough. You drink, but never have your fill. You put
on clothes, but are not warm. You earn wages, only to
put them in a purse with holes in it."* [Hag. 1:5–6]

Personalized license plates are a kind of social
commentary. While I don't have one on my car, I appreciate reading them. I've seen some doozies. Here are a few:

On the car of a police chief and his librarian wife: BOOKUM

On a Mustang convertible: TOPLESS

On a new Jaguar: IDZERVIT

On the car of a lady with allergies: AH CHOO

On a red Mercedes: HOT2TROT

On a car in Alaska: BRRRRR

On an evangelist's van: 100FOLD

On a car in a retirement community: O 2B 21

On a fisherman's truck: BASSMAN

On a fancy sports car: RUNVS

On an old junker: FASTONE

On a radiologist's bright sedan: I RAY D8

On a black Firebird: BATCAR

Most state license plates are limited to eight characters. One of my favorite personalized plates was seen on a New York car whose driver had a sharp sense of humor: PLANAHEA. Doesn't that say it all?

Enter Haggai. Can you imagine the nicknames this guy must have endured? Whatever the people of that day called him, Haggai was a wise planner. However, his audience was not. For instance, they worked and worked to earn more money, then put it in purses with holes. Their problem? Shortsightedness. They couldn't see beyond the "now." They had no rules for planning, no concept of order. Perhaps their shortsightedness showed most in that they expected no consequences for their sinful ways.

In his lighthearted book *Fumblerules,* that master of words William Safire takes a humorous look at the problems of grammar and good usage. He points out some of the careless blunders writers make by disobeying simple rules of composition. Safire illustrates these gaffs with "fumblerules"—errors that call attention to the grammatical principle they break. Here's a sample:

Avoid run-on sentences they are hard to read.

No sentence fragments.

It behooves us to avoid archaisms.

Also, avoid awkward or affected alliteration.

Don't use no double negatives.

If I've told you once, I've told you a thousand times: Resist hyperbole.

Avoid commas, that are not necessary.

Verbs has to agree with their subjects.

Avoid trendy locutions that sound flaky.

Writing carefully, dangling participles should not be used.

Kill all exclamation points!!!

Never use a long word when a diminutive one will do.

Proofread carefully to see if you any words out.

Take the bull by the hand, and don't mix metaphors.

Don't verb nouns.

Never, ever, use repetitive redundancies.

Last but not least, avoid cliches like the plague.

I hate to admit it, but I've broken most of these rules in my writing career. Sometimes because of poor planning, sometimes because of poor proofreading, but often to achieve a lighthearted, down-to-earth approach. (A few of the strict rules of usage don't always fit real communication.) But even the plans we make in life usually require proofreading and perfecting. Haggai's audience understood that point very well after the prophet delivered his message. Maybe Haggai told them the "fumblerules" of short-sightedness:

Poor planning brings pour results. Yes, I said "pour" results. When it rains it pours. Poor planning starts a hurricane of problems. It's like the old adage: "One lie leads to another." Pretty soon the liar has told lies about the lies and has to remember where the lies and truth crisscross just to keep the truth from being revealed. Bad plans always create a mess. Solution? Most people use patches. You know, Band-Aids. After enough mistakes crop up, the original plans are buried under a maze of mummy gauze. Haggai was telling the people: "Sin is a snake that always bites its owner. Pleasure for pleasure's sake never ends in pleasure. Investing in selfish success is a purse with holes. Look beyond today."

Expect the unexpected. Does that make sense? I mean, if something is unexpected, how could you possibly expect it? But shortsighted people usually expect their plans to go off without a hitch. How many times have I undertaken a household project with the noblest of goals, planning to finish quickly? A friend of mine once said: "When working on any project around the house, first calculate your time. Then add at least two hours." You may not be able to predict the specifics of the unexpected, but you should be ready for unpleasant surprises. Murphy's Law—"If anything can go wrong, it will"—didn't become a reality by accident. It's true. Especially true for those whose plans don't include God.

Avoiding failure doesn't qualify as success. I love what Ron Luciano asks in his book, *The Fall of the Roman Umpire:* "If you write a book entitled *How to Fail* and it fails, are you a success?" The shortsighted know little about genuine success. In their pursuit of mischief and shortcuts, they seldom consider what will result. If something goes awry, they simply take a different road, but in the same wrong direction. As poet Robert Burns put it, "The best laid schemes o' mice and men gang aft a-gley" (translation: "turn out like green cheese"). Those who include sin in their plans—operating under the delusion that all will be well—spend a lot of time looking at the road map. And since they usually carry a purse full of holes, they may not even have a dime for a phone call.

The wise planner looks past the lure of selfish, instant pleasure; the wise planner views today through the binoculars of eternity; the wise planner counts the letters before making a license plate; and the wise planner knows the fumblerules.

28 Reputation

The Bad and the Beautiful

This is what the LORD says: "I will return to Zion and dwell in Jerusalem. Then Jerusalem will be called the City of Truth, and the mountain of the LORD Almighty will be called the Holy Mountain." [Zech. 8:3]

Old Anonymous once said, "Reputation is what people *think* you to be, character is what God *knows* you to be." Maybe so, but that doesn't make reputation unimportant. Proverbs 22:1 tells us that "a good name is more desirable than great riches; to be esteemed is better than silver or gold." While we shouldn't live our lives merely to please others, neither should we ruin our good name by being detestable. A good reputation is still a valuable commodity.

Have you noticed that some people are known for certain things? Pick somebody famous. Let's say Michael Jordan. Air Jordan. Incredible leaps and spins with fabulous slam dunks. He's known for that. When fans go to see the Chicago Bulls basketball team, they expect to see the Michael Jordan Flying Circus.

Pick somebody else: Kim Basinger. A blonde for the '90s. Smart and sultry. Very worldly. A model of high fashion. Rich actress. Batman's girlfriend. That's what she's known for, good or bad. I wouldn't want those labels for my trademark, but it's more or less hers. A lot of young people admire Kim for just those things.

Some people have negative reputations. Some are known as untrustworthy scoundrels who would as soon tell you a lie as look at you. Some are known for their beastly manners. Some carry the label "Unreliable." Some have the reputation of being temperamental and violent. We learn to stigmatize people quickly (though sometimes unfairly). "Joe" parties wild and is a drunk. "Mary" sleeps around. "The Smiths" don't pay their bills. "Bill" cheats people or is always in trouble with the law. "Jane" is full of herself and hard to work with.

People can have positive reputations, too. Some are especially known for their kindness and fairness. Who is the best Christian you know? I can name a handful of folks who exemplify the qualities of Christ. That is their legacy. Good people are known for their ways—thoughtfulness, generosity, neighborliness, for example. "Betty" always has a smile and a pleasant attitude. "Al" is a hard worker, valuable to the company. "The Johnsons" are such a happy couple and have a strong marriage.

Reputation isn't limited to individuals. Businesses have a "good name" to uphold. Restaurants can have good food, poor service, lousy management, terrific decor, an unusual menu, music that's too loud, dirty facilities, lavish restrooms, small portions, a huge salad bar, a lovely view, a specialty to die for. Clothing stores can have cheap merchandise, good sales, unfriendly sales clerks, a large selection, excellent customer service, ratty dressing rooms, fair prices. In any successful business, the good labels must speak much louder than the bad ones.

Nearly everything and everybody has some kind of reputation. The school on the corner has a drug problem. Doctor Barnes is a quack. Such-and-such company has terrible long-distance phone service. The grocery store down the street has the freshest produce, but the one four blocks away has a better meat counter. Coke is better than Pepsi. This college is tops for journalism, that one is best for law. That woman is a great mother. That hospital overcharges its patients.

Humans like to use tags. Granted, first impressions can be misleading, so we shouldn't be quick to pass judgment. We should usually give people a second chance and a third. But let's talk reality for a moment. We can work toward the ideal once we know the real score. Reality is this: We humans draw conclusions, fair and unfair, based on what we see and hear about others.

Furthermore, you may be a really great person, but your "bad" qualities—the labeling often based solely on any questionable places you may sometimes frequent and the companions you choose—will register faster with others than your good ones. We all know that tabloid writers thrive on this human fascination with scandal and malicious rumors, many of them unsubstantiated by fact. Obviously, then, although maybe 20 percent of the people you meet won't like you no matter what you do, outward appearances count for a lot, even when they don't represent the real you. A good reputation is a priceless asset; a bad one is fairly easy to come by, but it is very costly in terms of human relationships and hard to erase on a balance sheet.

As we check out what the prophet Zechariah has to say, we notice he illustrates the importance of reputation by telling the Israelites that their beloved Jerusalem will *one day* be called the City of Truth, the Holy Mountain. If you scan Mr. Z's earlier words, though, you would find that Jerusalem's reputation has suffered quite a bit. God is trying to get them to sharpen up their act. Here are two points worth pondering on the subject of "What's in a Name?"

It takes time to build a good reputation. Jerusalem isn't going to have its prized name—City of Truth—without adversity and struggle and some house cleaning. Neither can you have a good name without applying yourself to high standards. If you don't care what people think of you, don't be surprised if they think the worst. To be sure, you can't conform to everyone else's idea of what you should be. But beware of intentionally rejecting reasonable ideas of conformity for the sake of proving that no one can interfere with your independence. It is also good to remember that a house that took many days to build can burn down in a few hours. Carefully guard your reputation, as if you were defending your life. That's how important it is.

You can change your reputation. Have you made a bad name for yourself? So what! It doesn't have to stay that way. Bring in new management. Put Jesus in charge. He has the ability to make crooked things straight. Of course, it will require effort and patience on your part. The onlookers might be suspicious for a while. If standing for something positive and meaningful is important to you—which I hope it is—you can clean up your name with God's help.

First you have to see yourself as others do. If that's not a pretty picture, start painting a new one.

What's in a name? A "rose" is not necessarily a rose; it may be a weed. Be sure the label you're wearing is the correct one, or at least strip away the thorns.

Prophecies
of Heart

Malachi

A man who works with his hands is a laborer. A man who works with his hands and his brain is a craftsman. But a man who works with his hands and his brain and his heart is an artist.

Anonymous

Hearts are flowers; they remain open to the softly falling dew, but shut up in the violent downpour of rain.

Jean Paul Richter

29 Blasphemy

White Hunter, Black Heart

"But you profane it by saying of the Lord's table, 'It is defiled,' and of its food, 'It is contemptible.' And you say, 'What a burden!' and you sniff at it contemptuously," says the LORD Almighty. "When you bring injured, crippled or diseased animals and offer them as sacrifices, should I accept them from your hands?" says the LORD. [Mal. 1:12–13]

I once heard a story about a young evangelist who was preaching near the student center of a college campus. Quite a crowd gathered to hear him proclaim God's existence and the doctrines of creation. He excitedly expounded on the wonders of the Genesis account, explaining how God created all things in six days and rested on the seventh. He sharply denounced the humanistic theory of evolution. Such a message is bound to ruffle feathers on the campus scene.

Suddenly, from the midst of the gathering, a heckler challenged the young preacher. "If there's a God, prove it."

"There's proof all around you. Just look," he replied as he motioned to some nearby flowers and shrubs.

"Really?" the heckler's tone dripped with sarcasm. Then, after a pause, he sought to rile the evangelist with profanities: "@#@$! you and your stupid God, too. There is no God."

That stirred some interest among the students who, like most of us, are attracted to a good fight. The crowd began to grow. Much whispering went on as the spiritual debate continued.

"God loves you, whether or not you believe he exists," said the evangelist.

"You fool, there is no God," persisted the heckler.

"You seem so sure of that, why don't you prove to me and this whole crowd that God does not exist. You want me to prove that he does; I ask you to prove that he doesn't."

The crowd was enjoying this match, but they seemed to be on the side of the evangelist because of his gentle demeanor.

"Fine. I can prove that," the skeptic said as he stepped onto the low wall where the evangelist was standing. Waving his arms around and hollering, the heckler said, "If there's a God, let him send an earthquake in the next minute. Let him just shake up this whole place."

"Very well," the evangelist responded, "and if there is a God—which I certainly believe there is—let him have mercy on every one of us, including you, and not send an earthquake at all."

The crowd loved the evangelist's counter-remark. Laughter rippled through the audience, mixed with scattered applause. The debate was ended. The heckler stalked off, cursing and flashing obscene gestures toward heaven.

Blasphemy comes in many disguises less obvious than the heathenistic outrage of taking God's name in vain. Is it not blasphemy when satanic musicians sing the glories of evil and use their God-given talent to revel in wickedness? Is it not blasphemy when our government disallows the teaching of creation as an alternative theory to evolution, but continues to permit the exclusive influence of secular humanism? Is it not blasphemy when some mainline denominational leaders allow practicing homosexuals to be ordained into the gospel ministry and sanction homosexual "marriages" in a travesty of what God intended?

I believe we tiptoe across the borders of blasphemy anytime we exchange the truth for a lie. Malachi was a first-hand witness to that very problem in his day. The temple-goers in Malachi's parish had religion down to a science. They saved big bucks by using weak and sickly animals for their holy sacrifices. Their attitude said, "This worship thing is such a drag. Let's just give our little donation and get out of here."

The blasphemy of Malachi's day reminds me of the searching words Cheryl Forbes wrote in her interesting work, *The Religion of Power:*

We are so concerned to show the world what a good life Christians have, and thus to prove to them that they should join up, that we have decided that the end absolutely justifies the means. And the means is power. Christian organizations spend a lot of money, time, talent, imagination, and energy each year for power. We may call it witnessing, we may call it influence, we may call it using modern technology for Christ's sake. That veneer is certainly present. A scratch will show the veneer for what it is.

Pow! What a point. Churches do a lot of things in the name of religion that haven't an ounce of spiritual meat to them. I am ashamed to admit that too many religious leaders today are more interested in politics than saving souls, more consumed with their own power than with peace for all. When we so corrupt the gospel—the perfect love that Jesus showed by dying for our sins—what makes us different from the heathen who scoffs at God? Like the diseased calves Malachi called "contemptible," we should call this jazz by its name: blasphemy. Whew! Throw some cold water on me, and pull me down from this soapbox.

"Wow, Earles," you may be wondering, "you're pretty strict on this blasphemy thing aren't you?" Maybe so, but I truly believe God wants us to know the truth and keep it pure and simple. That truth is clearly stated in the Bible, and it's unchangeable and incontrovertible. But any skeptics—those "I need a sign" guys and gals—need only look around them for further evidence. That, too, is plain enough! God will not allow his truth to be corrupted. If we try to play fast and loose with God's gospel and with his love, his power, and his character, how do you think he views that?

Don't mistake God's silence to mean that he doesn't notice and doesn't care. God doesn't always send an earthquake to prove his point. And it shouldn't be necessary!

30 Regrets

Gone with the Wind

Another thing you do: You flood the LORD's altar with tears. You weep and wail because he no longer pays attention to your offerings or accepts them with pleasure from your hands. [Mal. 2:13]

Barry Levinson, a famous Hollywood director, took a chance many of his colleagues passed up. They thought the script about an autistic middle-aged man and his younger brother was too much of a drag for sophisticated American audiences. Levinson saw potential, though. He liked the interaction between the brothers. With the

167

able assistance of actors Dustin Hoffman and Tom Cruise, Levinson crafted a beautiful tale of humor and drama. Hoffman's classic depiction of Raymond Babbitt won him an Academy Award. The film *Rain Man* went on to gross over five hundred million dollars. Talk about regrets! I'm sure there is a handful of directors and producers who wish they could have that script back.

This gaffer wasn't the first ever by moviemakers. The Sad Producers Club has many other members. Take MGM executive Irving Thalberg, who told Louis B. Mayer, "No Civil War picture ever made a nickel." One *Gone With the Wind* later, Irv was looking a little pale and rival Dave Selznick was smugly raking in the bucks. Or how about the Hollywood executive who blushes to remember his review of a certain skinny dancer's screen test: "Can't act. Slightly bald. Also dances." He missed his opportunity to sign up Fred Astaire.

John Greenleaf Whittier, one of our most astute poets, wrote: "For of all the sad words of tongue or pen,/ The saddest are these: 'It might have been.'" That's what regret is all about. The world is full of people who regret having thoughtlessly chosen the wrong path. Life is a series of forks in the road, some more important than others, of course. But the choices are up to us. And the consequences of those choices belong to us, too. (Remember chapter 24?)

I don't know one person who hasn't made at least one blunder that resulted in personal regret. Each of us can look back on an event we'd like to do over. I don't mean to disillusion you, but mistakes—even sinfulness—are inevitable for us mortals. That doesn't permit us to be deliberate imitators of the prodigal. The "major" here is not that we can be perfect; it's that we should learn the art of recovering from bad moves.

Even Bible heroes mourned their deplorable memories of wrongdoing. The apostle Paul must have had painful remembrances of watching Stephen crumple beneath the vicious stoning that took his life. It was Paul—as Saul the persecutor—who had held the killers' coats. Though he was later a magnificent servant of Jesus Christ, he often recalled his former days as a tormentor of Christians.

There were many others with cause for regret, including Abraham and Sarah, who laughed at God's promises. And Elijah (another important prophet, though his works are not contained in a single book), who destroyed Israel's idols on one day and high-tailed it in fear of Jezebel on the next. And there was King David, who committed adultery with Bathsheba. And Absalom, David's son, who rebelled against his father. And Lot, who wasted precious years living in Sodom. And Peter, who denied the Savior at the hour of his crucifixion. The line of regretters goes back to Adam, who disobeyed the one simple command God gave him.

Malachi observed the agony of regret, the absolute remorse of an entire people who had lost their way. His words have a familiar ring to all us travelers who walk the road of grace in a broken world: "You flood the LORD's altar with tears. You weep and wail because he no longer pays attention to your offerings or accepts them with pleasure from your hands." There's no pain so intense as feeling God's disappointment and of wishing you could turn back the clock. Here's a "major" no textbook teaches, but its truths should be carved in stone:

Decisions need the counsel of prayer. All my worst choices have one thing in common: I never prayed over them. As a matter of fact, my most regrettable decisions were acts of willful disobedience. I was afraid to pray over them, because I knew they were wrong. Listen to the grief in Malachi's words. You don't want that kind of misery. So

169

pray over your decisions. You will never regret seeking God's direction for your life.

Wrong paths can be changed. It's not as easy as snapping your fingers and Poof! all is well, but praise God for second chances. When the prodigal grew homesick, he knew the way back, though the trip was long and the hills high. Many miles rolled beneath his feet before he felt his father's kiss. And I imagine he never wanted to see a pig again. Paul said that it was wrong for Christians to sin just to see grace abound (Rom. 6:1). And yet, because grace *does* abound, we can repent, receive forgiveness, and make a fresh start. Be careful, however, not to develop the attitude that it's easy to file for spiritual bankruptcy and start over. If you do too much of that, you won't have much to show for your life—and bad habits are mighty tough to break.

Regrets play a role in shaping our faith and our lives. I need my past. Really. Don't get me wrong. If I had the opportunity to do some things over, I'd jump at it. When some of my darker moments cast a shadow over my thoughts, I can feel my face tingling with deep red embarrassment. No one is looking, only my conscience. The wayward child in me kicks himself for being so dumb. Long after the salve of forgiveness has healed the open wound, the scar still feels tender. But I've taken note of a remarkable irony: Sometimes God gently touches me there. It's as if he's saying, "Remember how that happened, son? Remember the day you took back the keys to your heart? Aren't you much happier here with me? Life is a lot simpler at my side, isn't it?" In those moments, when we are alone together, I feel overwhelmed by his mercy. I feel so loved and so glad that he came all that way to rescue me. I'd rather not have the regrets, but I am so thankful for the forgiveness. Being nothing more than a sinner, I am grateful for the healing.

170

Toward the end of *Rain Man,* Charlie (Tom Cruise) begins to regret that he didn't grow up knowing Raymond. Then a touching exchange of affection occurs between the brothers: Charlie teaches Raymond to dance. It is Charlie's opportunity to recapture something he missed. I am so glad Jesus taught me to dance.

OVERLY SERIOUS? WHO SAYS WE CHRISTIANS ARE OVERLY SERIOUS? THIS IS AN OUTRAGE! IT'S PERSECUTION I TELL YOU!

31 Playtime

Butterflies Are Free

But for you who revere my name, the sun of righteousness will rise with healing in its wings. And you will go out and leap like calves released from the stall. [Mal. 4:2]

One of my favorite books is Tim Hansel's *When I Relax I Feel Guilty.* He really hits me between the eyes with his indictment of Christians caught in the trap of being overly serious. Listen to his insight:

Play is more than just nonwork. It is one of the pieces in the puzzle of our existence, a place for our excesses and exuberances. It is where life lives in a very special way. It is the time when we forget our problems for a while and remember who we are. Play is more than just a game. It is where you recognize again the supreme importance of life itself. Like a child, you see life as it is and as it was meant to be. In play you can abandon yourself, you can immerse yourself without restraint, you can pierce life's complexities and confusions. You can be whole again without trying.

Wow! That's good stuff. I expect some believers think that play and Christianity have no place together, but the two actually blend very well. Can you imagine the disciples running along the shores of Galilee, enjoying life? Or do you suppose they always just sat around, pondering the deep issues of theology? Do you think they ever laughed or played? Sure they did. They were real people who lived real lives. Maybe they skipped stones across the water or went for a long morning run together on the sandy beach. Perhaps they had target practice with slingshots. Scripture doesn't give any details, but they needed escape from the pressures of the world just like we all do.

Scripture is full of admonishments telling us to be joyful. The joy of the Lord is our strength (Neh. 8:10). It is evidence that the Holy Spirit is at work in our lives (Gal. 5:22). In fact, in the Galatians passage, Paul seems to imply that there is no love or peace without joy. The "fruit of the Spirit" has several ingredients. Joy is one of them. Unless joy is present, there is no real love, no real peace, no real faithfulness.

Somehow I find it hard to believe that long-faced, serious-minded, deep-thinking Christianity is all Jesus has to offer. Remember, he promised abundant life to his followers. He is the one who said, "My yoke is easy and my burden is light" (Matt. 11:30).

Even Jesus doesn't strike me as the all-work-no-play type. I truly believe he knew the pleasure of relaxing. He slipped away to the mountains occasionally. And once, when his disciples were all astir because of a raging storm, Jesus slept peacefully in the bottom of the boat. Don't get me wrong. I'm not minimizing the earnest ministry of our Savior. He was always about his Father's business. Just the same, I believe he would attend a baseball game with me if he were here and I asked him. He might enjoy a hot dog and share the gospel with everyone in our section. Hey, I'm not being sacrilegious. I just think Jesus understands us and life better than we understand him and what spiritual living really means.

Like multitudes of others, I have chased ambition and competition and success only to trigger the spring and get squashed. It reminds me of the mouse who said, "I don't want the cheese, I just want to get out of the trap." You may be surprised to hear that playtime is one way out of the trap.

Malachi paints a fun word picture in the verse that leads our chapter. He says that those who revere the name of God will jump around like calves just released from the stall. Healing comes to those people, and so does playfulness. He must have known the verse that says, "A cheerful heart is good medicine" (Prov. 17:22). Play is the ready antidote for depression. Learn how to play, graduate, instead of learning how to be sick.

There are many different kinds of play. It does not matter which ones you choose. Whether it's a game, a good book, a stamp collection, a weight machine, or gourmet cooking, play is a time to draw aside from the toil of life. It is your opportunity to be refreshed and beat the apathy that is destroying others. It is your chance at discovering the joyful life.

174

Before I finish talking about life's majors and minors, I want to emphasize the vital need for this particular one. I'm not suggesting wild, reckless abandon. If you've read the other chapters, you know me better than that. But life is supposed to be fun, not excruciating pain. Take lessons in fun. There is plenty of stress in life to keep you serious.

In his book *This Running Life*, George Sheehan describes the essence of achieving balance and fulfillment in a mixed-up world:

> The tinfoil collectors and the fancy ribbon savers may be absurd, but they're not crazy. They are the ones who still retain the capacity for wonder that is the root of caring. When a little boy finds an old electric motor on a junk heap, he is pierced to the heart by the weight, the windings, and the silent turning of it. When he gets home, his mother tells him to throw it out. Most likely he will cry. It is his first and truest reaction to the affluent society. He usually forgets it, but we shouldn't. He is sane; society isn't. He possesses because he cares. We don't.

Don't discard the simple pleasures of life. Learn to play. It is a major you can spend a lifetime using and enjoying. What college or profession can promise you that? Step joyfully into a bustling universe and live an abundant life.